JACOB'S LADDER

JACOB'S LADDER

∂

Paradise Regained

by Michele Longo O'Donnell

LA VIDA PRESS
SAN ANTONIO

Library of Congress Cataloging
in Publication Data

ISBN 9781495205224 softcover

Published in 2014 by
La Vida Press
107 Scenic Loop Road
Boerne, Texas 78006
830-755-8767

Cover design and illustration by Travis Ward

Printed in USA

Other writings and materials by
MICHELE LONGO O'DONNELL

BOOKS:

"Of Monkeys and Dragons:
                 Freedom From the Tyranny of Disease"

"The God That We've Created: The Basic Cause of All Disease"

"When the Wolf is at the Door: The Simplicity of Healing"

"Only Receive: No Barriers, No Bounderies"

"Unspeakable Mercy"

Daily Devotionals:
"Arise Shine: For Your Time Has Come" Volume 1

"Arise Shine: For Your Time Has Come" Volume 2

CD's:

Multitudes of ....
Individual Teachings
Teaching Series
Annual Retreat Series

For more information: www.livingbeyonddisease.com
or www.micheleodonnell.com

As always the premature death of my beloved sister and brother-in-law drove home to my heart the need for a whole new perception of life on the earth. This revealed, and totally liberting understanding, is here for our accepting. Divine Love would have it no other way. So once again I dedicate this book, as I have with each of my writings,
to Peggy and Ray...
and to all those who desperately need to understand.

Psalm 90:1,2
"Lord you have been our dwelling place in all
generations before the mountains were brought
forth and before the foundation of the earth was
laid, even from everlasting to everlasting...."

Job 38:4,7
Where were you when I laid the foundations of
the earth and when the morning stars sang together, and all the sons of God shouted for joy?

Ephesians1:3,4
Blessed be God who has chosen us in Him before
the foundation of the world, holy and without
blame before Him in love.

Tao is an ancient Chinese, metaphysical term signifying the primordial essence or fundamental nature of the universe...the underlying natural order of the universe.

The American Indians referred to this Source of all existence, running throughout all that is visible, maintaining and sustaining it all, as the Great Spirit.

For this work, I will refer to it as the Eternal Spirit of Life. It is Creative intelligence, wisdom, balance, order, harmony, self sustaining and utterly immutable. To enter into the flow of it is life itself. To awaken to its Presence within you is Eternal Life.

"When the great Tao is forgotten,
goodness and piety appear."
Tao Te Ching

"For the ONE who has become many,
(yet) remains the ONE undivided,
but each part is all of Christ."
Saint Simeon, the Younger
949 AD

TABLE OF CONTENTS

ACKNOWLEDGEMENTS

How could such a book be written without the living, breathing Spirit of Wisdom and Eternal Life guiding, directing, and influencing every thought? This had become my constant companion, my intention for living, my ability to do anything. And I wouldn't have it any other way.

So it has appeared as my friend Melissa, who tirelessly edits and then edits again and again. She is the wealth of information and "how to get anything done" in my life.

My friend, Kay, a constant source of support and encouragement, who always shows up when I need help the most.

My friend, Lee, who knows every scripture I refer to and is the source of the in-depth footnotes and scripture references you will find here.

And to everyone who has shown up along my way who has added Wisdom and Understanding to my soul.

Thank you all.

CHAPTER ONE

INTRODUCTION TO
LIVING BEYOND DISEASE

The ministry of Living Beyond Disease has always had one focus, one goal and one vision. And that is enabling others to experience a paradigm shift of consciousness that is very necessary if we are to finally live our time here without the threat of, the fear of, or the actual experience of dis-ease. Or any pain, lack, loss, failure or the like. To live the glorious Life that was ours from "before the foundation of the world."[1] To live superior to all painful human conditions that may present themselves to us for recognition and validity. To live the Jesus Christ Life as he declared we should.

To do this we must clean the slate, so to speak, and start all over again in perception and understanding; led not by the dictates of the human mind, led not by the dictates of religion's many and convoluted ideologies, led not by modern medical madness, and led not by our body's feelings or demands...but by the impulse of the Spirit of Truth given to us by Jesus (John 14:26, 15:13) to lead and guide us into all truth. We must learn to see out from the heart of God, whose heart beats in our own chest. What does that feel like? What does God see? What does he know? What does life look like coming from the Infinite Divine Mind? What is his intention and expectation for us? Can it be achieved here on earth? Is it designed to be experienced now? Or off on some futuristic date and time? Jesus said that we should pray to know these answers, for it is said that we should experience this, "on earth as it is in heaven."[2] Revelation promises a new experience here on earth when it speaks of a new heaven and a new earth.[3] All the old ideas and unquestioned beliefs and expectations must be swallowed up by a new perception and expectation. We must begin to fearlessly live life, the Life designed for us.

We are a disease ridden society. We are covered by an unchallenged expectation of disease as a mass consciousness. We are so entrenched in this that, instead of stepping back and asking "why," we spend our time frantically trying to find yet another pill to subdue whatever has appeared on the horizon of medical hysteria. We have changed the truth of God into a lie by accepting all this and by declaring that it is God who purposed this for our good. We hear such empty nonsense as, "we will understand after we die," or, "it must have been God's will. We must have deserved it or needed it for a purpose in the future." All this declares the depths of our ignorance...both of the truth of who and what we are, and of the nature and intentions of God. We create a god who just doesn't exist. Then we pass it all onto our dear children, "passing them through the fires of Molech,"[4] sacrificing them to this strange god we erected in our minds, causing them to draw or attract unto themselves what is then unconsciously held in their belief system.

And as for learning this in the "sweet by and by," why not now when we need to know it in order to live? Yet in the midst of all the goofy words spoken throughout the ages the voice of Spirit still roars its eternal truth, "Unto us it is given to know the mysteries of the kingdom of God."[5] This is why Jesus gave us (actually opened up within us) the Spirit of Truth, to deliver us from the chains and shackles of our present thought. Further it says, "It is the Glory of God to conceal a thing, but it is the honor of kings to search it out."[6] And we are "made unto him Kings and priests"[7] that we might reign with him forever and ever.

When I was 17 years old and suffering through my first day as a student nurse I saw things that were so horrifying to me, so much human suffering, so much fear and despair as one could stand to look upon. I had no idea that people suffered like that! Disease was not a focus of conversation at our home although we had our fair share of sickness now and then. But what really struck me that life-changing day...not only the misery and injustice of it all...but that no one seemed to challenge its right to exist! All the attention was directed to what humanly could be done for whatever appeared...as if everyone just accepted that this was a necessary part of the human existence! Was I the only one who thought the whole thing needed to be done away with? The injustice of it all! What was it all about? Why did we allow it to exist in the first place? I watched as doctors, nurses, patients and families marched on as if in a trance under the influence of something so unnecessary, so devastating. And no one uttered a complaint! Where was the outrage?

I never spoke these words to anyone because there was no one who I believed might feel the same way. Everyone was just busy trying to learn about all the diseases and what was on the horizon of care those days. Was anyone else screaming inside, "No. no. no! This is all wrong!" Needless to say this thought never left me. You see, on that day something happened to me. I found myself "outside" of the hysteria and madness all around me, as if I was but a beholder, an observer of the whole scenario. I watched it all but all the while I "knew" something very different. I knew it was not just all wrong, but that it was going to end. I knew that in my lifetime I would see a world completely devoid of disease and such suffering, such victimhood, such subservience to evil. I knew then to speak this was crazy, just as people might think so even now. But many people throughout history have "seen" things and known things that were crazy to the average observer. And they stuck to their certainty. And at some point the human perception changed and what they knew became a reality for all. Anyway, I didn't expect this. I didn't ask for this. But I have lived my life as though it already was, because I have been compelled to do so.

The clearest advice I can offer in embracing this vision is this: When a building is erected and it turns out to be unstable and unsafe and all wrong what do we do? If we're smart we will go back to the blueprint and study it, tear down the old and begin all over again. We might have to let the old contractor go (religious traditions, past and present human experiences) and hire a new one (Holy Spirit).

The answer to it all is a newer, clearer, and truer concept of God, the Creator of it all. To go back to the Source, the blue print, we go back to the nature of God. Leaving behind whatever we have been taught and going forth with a heart that doesn't care where our search takes us or how it will all turn out... just so that it is real and true and eternal. And the first thing we find, much to our eternal amazement, is that God is only good. We learn that "each seed reproduces after its own kind"[8] and since there is only one Creator, one Source, that makes everything that comes forth from this Source of Life only good. Genesis, chapter 1, tells us that when God looked at what he created, he said "It is very good!" Here, in the Hebrew translation, we find the word good means incorruptible, indestructible, immutable (unchanging) and perfect. And this is where we must start.

God warned us not to partake of the knowledge of good and evil, or we would die.[9] And yet we declare that both good and evil come from God. So does he partake of what he said would cause us to die? This corrupted image of God must be challenged. But be cautioned...never look at human mortal appearances (human suffering, disease, death, etc) and try to determine the truth of God. That would be like looking at $2 + 2 = 5$ and then trying to build the entire world of mathematics around an error. Don't start by agreeing with this horrible picture and then trying to come up with a God that fits this picture! No! Instead look at what is true about God, eternally true and never changes, and insist on the picture, the image, the visible appearance changing to fit what is eternally true. "While we look not at those things which are temporal but upon those things which are eternal. For the temporal things will fade away but the eternal is forever."[10]

So God is the only Creator. And all that is visible came forth from him. Each seed is a blue print of its parent, and since God is Good his creation is also pure, perfect, untouchable and uninterrupted. "The earth magnifies the Glory of God.[11] "We are his masterpiece, created in perfection."[12] Jesus said that "According to what we believed so shall we experience!"[13] If we believed this and knew it was true, we would see our experience changing before our eyes. Proverbs, the book of eternal Wisdom, declares that "as a man thinketh in his heart, so is he."[14] What we stare at, focus upon, look at day and night is what we experience. So we are instructed to never look away from his face (image, nature), no matter what is clamoring for our attention.

God is Life eternal. Not just the Source of Life, but Life itself. The pulsating flow of dynamic, electrifying vitality. It is alive with joy unspeakable, love and laughter. It is cognizant of its own magnificent being, only. It rushes throughout eternity or it casually and steadily streams along, whatever its pleasure. And out from its very being it causes the visible to appear. Life appearing as living organisms, all showing forth the nature of its parent being. God making himself visible to all who will choose to see. Romans tells us that "the invisible things of him are clearly seen and understood by that which has been made."[15] Psalms 19 boldly declares, "The heavens declare the glory of God and the firmament shows forth his handiwork. Day unto day utters speech and night unto night shows knowledge. There is no language on earth where their voice is not heard."[16] All of creation, when seen in all of its uncontaminated beauty and glory does show forth the entirety of God.

The fullness of this is Eternal Life. God therefore is Eternal Life.

"This life is the light of men."[17]

"This is the true light that lights every man born into the world."[18]

"And of his fullness have we all received!"[19]

And when men are made aware of this, all sense of sin and condemnation and failure and need for suffering is gone. Disease then must vanish back into its "native nothingness." Just as $2 \times 2 = 5$ vanishes when it is known and understood that 2×2 indeed equals 4.

We do not need to earn this Life. This is not a journey to become something that we are not already. We are even now one with this Life. It is our very own Life.[20]

We are as eternal as the Life that formed us by his word of intention.

We vibrate in accord with the Source which pulsates through us. Our life and his life are one and the same, as we submerge ourselves into this reality. We forget the nonsense of suffering. We forget the myriad of voices declaring the power and reality of disease.

We forget the insanity of religion as it forces us into believing we must earn Eternal Life by suffering, and then maybe receive it after we die. Maybe!

Here it is and here we are, and we are one with eternal Life.

CHAPTER TWO

PARADISE REGAINED

We live in an invisible space called paradise, the garden of God. One in which he is the designer, maintainer and sustainer... and this is an eternal, uninterrupted, immutable fact of existence. It is and has always been our true residence.

It is said that two fish swam by each other in the ocean and one greeted the other with, "The water is wonderful, isn't it!" The second fish looked bewildered and asked, "What is water?" We have walked and talked, laughed and loved and lived out our days in this exquisite place called paradise but like the second fish, and although it is all around us, we have missed it completely.

Deep within the center of this garden (a consciousness of pure beauty, order and richness of all that is to be desired) is the Source of all Life, symbolically called the Tree of Life. In Revelation, chapter 2, verse 7, we read, "To him that overcomes (actually means to come up over what is currently believed) I will give to eat of the tree of life which is in the midst of the paradise of God." It is freely there for us to eat so that we may fully enjoy the peace and abundance, the indescribable richness of joy and delight that is experienced when there is no knowledge of evil, fear, pain, loss or lack. This is a place uncontaminated by religion's dreadful voice of sin, failure, suffering and death.

We must learn of this Life if we are to live the life of goodness provided for us. We must learn how to partake of it...and how we have missed it as well.

Here the birds sing out with the richness of abandoned glee as they soar overhead. The animals and creatures roam content with their provisions. The creatures bask in the sunlight never knowing the frantic scurrying of ceaselessly looking for food, for all that is needed is supplied before the need is realized. The lion lies down with the lamb. Here there is nothing known of greed for gain, competiveness or a personal sense of responsibility to survive. Here creation simply receives and enjoys with great gratitude, for the giver of it all is their Creator. And his name is Love.

Just as a fish dies outside its environment of water, so do we also die outside of the safety and security of our home environment. Outside of paradise is called the knowledge of good and evil. It is dark out there and chaotic. Confusion reigns. There is hurrying and scurrying, a wild franticness as each creature seeks its own good. It is filled with crying, despair, wild imagined fears that materialize into unfulfilled wants, needs and desires. Jesus refers to this as "outer darkness where there is only weeping and gnashing of teeth and devouring one another."[21]

The mind is void of Life. The thoughts are insane, with no order, no sense, and nonproductive. There is no gratitude, no voice of thanksgiving because everyone has assumed the role of self provider. To whom then would they give thanks? The restlessness, the emptiness, each one trying unsuccessfully to fill the void in their souls, finally results in disease of the body. The body is a result of the consciousness that holds it. If the space lived in is chaotic, the body begins to appear chaotic. Disease, no matter the proud and lofty names attached to it, is yet only disorder, confusion. When order and peace is regained, the body begins to appear in perfect order. Conversely, if the space we choose to live in is the well watered garden of God, the body is at rest and all is well.

Jesus taught us this by healing on the Sabbath, much to the chagrin of the empty, religious voice of his day. Sabbath means the "rest of God." His teaching points us back to the rest, the peace, the place where we are loved and cared for once again. Here the appearance will be wholeness, for only in this state of surety and contentment can wholeness be realized. (read Hebrews, chapters 3 and 4...also Isaiah, chapter 58, vs. 13 and 14)

Religion tells us that we have lost this place and we will never find it again until we die. Jesus says it is here within you right now. Never lost but only forgotten. Religion tells us that we must suffer to regain this place. Jesus says that by faith we enter in...and that by grace (his overflowing Presence of the Spirit of Life).

The faithful Cherubim, holding a flaming sword and guarding the "entrance" to this garden[22] is really our hope. Contrary to the upside down vision and devoid understanding of religion. The angel was not placed there to keep us out but to burn away the horror of religion's ugly voice and all its confusion and condemnation **so that we could reenter.**

One by one the traditions of men, the doctrines of religion, the proud, mindless medical declarations of absolute nonsense, must be purged away for us to freely enter in. And the good news is that God does this for us. We are not responsible to do it for ourselves. For we cannot. Einstein said that the same consciousness that created the problem can never correct itself. A new consciousness, a new understanding must be realized. New wine cannot be put into old wineskins.[23] So again the good news is that God does this for us. "For behold, I will pour out my Spirit (the fullness of my very being, my Life) upon ALL flesh and ALL shall know me (not man's definition of me, but MY definition of me)...from the least to the greatest. Your sins and iniquities shall I remember no more."[24] That means we shall not remember any of the old realm of failure, sin and suffering. It will be swallowed up, covered, by the joy, the delight, the sense of pure abundant goodness.

Stop here and consider what life might feel like with all sense of fear, dread and failure absent. Imagine what wonder and joy would you enter into if you heard the Spirit speak to your soul, "From this day forward you shall not fear or experience evil...your dreams and hopes shall appear to your joy...you shall not know failure again." We shall be filled with whatever this wonderful Spirit of truth, Spirit of life pours into our understanding. Further He says,

"I will CAUSE you to follow my way, the WAY OF LIFE. You will not need to grope or crawl along in confusion any longer, for I will carry you."

Now when does this event happen? Right here, right now. Just as soon as you lift your heart to heaven and cry out for your paradise to reappear to you.

This Paradise, this Garden of Eden is called Eternal Life. This then is a journey from one conscious awareness to another, from the "death" produced by the knowledge of good vs. evil, to the life secured by the knowledge of Eternal Life...and it is now, and ever has been...and you are the result of its existence.

CHAPTER THREE

ETERNAL LIFE

What exactly is this "gift of eternal life?" It seems to be the goal of every religion. But what is it? If it is a gift from God, is it freely given or are there strings attached? Is it something outside of us, added to us, or is it already deep within waiting to be experienced? Is it for everyone or for just the chosen few? Is it for now or after we pass from this life? After we have earned it? After we have suffered enough to deserve it...if, in fact, suffering is a prerequisite?

Is this earthly experience a proving ground, as so many say? Are we constantly being tested? If we pass we get to experience whatever this Eternal Life really is...but if we fail will we never know what we missed?

The true answers to these questions, fully understood and embraced, will yield a life free from pain, sorrow, suffering, disease, loss, conflict and evil of any sort, right here on earth. This is why Eternal Life is the greatest gift of God.

The gift is actually the awakening to what is available here and now. It is not giving us something we don't have, but allowing us to experience it...now when it is needed the most.

This is why we must seek to understand its true meaning. And in order to do this we must be willing to challenge every teaching and thought of Eternal Life that has ever been spoken throughout the generations of men. It is impossible to learn anything new if you are convinced you already know it. Humility. The brokenness of heart and soul that cries out for understanding is the only thing we can bring to this banquet table of Infinite Love. "In all your getting, get wisdom and understanding."[25] Not from men. Not from doctrines and traditions. Not from religions of the world. But from God, himself. The giver of the gift. God, the Gift itself.

The complacent of heart will never know this. A lukewarm condition is "poor, wretched, blind and naked."[26] It is content to remain with what is comfortable, even when proven wrong.

But to those who seek, to those who feel a constant tugging, sometimes a roaring in their souls that will not be silenced, the answer...and the bountiful life that awaits your understanding...will surely come.

There are two distinct views and perceptions of life, one commonly held by man, taught of man. The other would be that unveiled understanding which is known of God and which can only be taught of God. Which one we choose will determine the conditions of our personal experiences while we live here on earth. We do not live and experience life by a roll of the dice, the law of chance. We do not live by a predetermined, predestined intention either. We do not live by our ancestors or by our DNA, which is proven to change with changing emotions and expectations! WE LIVE AND EXPERIENCE ACCORDING TO WHAT WE BELIEVE TO BE TRUE.

Eternal Life is a blueprint of life as known in the heart of God. Freely shared if we seek it. And the best news of all...it is freely lived out for us, through us! Once we learn of this, we can't go wrong.

Can you image how infinitely wonderful life can be by simply allowing God to reveal and teach us his LIFE? If you have taken the time to really seek God until HE defined his true nature to you, (which IS Eternal Life) you would find a love so pure, so intense, so consistent that you would not be the least afraid to trust it with your life. You would find this love never depended upon your performance to experience it. You would feel safe, secure and unafraid of "sudden destruction"[27] appearing.

This love so directed toward you, and filling your own soul, would make you feel pure, clean, untouched by corruption or failure. Totally innocent. Guiltless. You would feel worthy to be so loved. It would make you love everyone just as you are loved. You would expect every good thing to come to you without being demanding or greedy. There would be no need for aggression or self defense. There would be nothing to defend one's self from.

Never again would you believe that evil could, or would, come from God. You would know it was the result of what was humanly being believed, but never could God be the progenitor of such sadness or destruction. To do so he would need to deny his own love nature. His goodness turns us from our wayward ways, so there is never a need for punishment. "It is the goodness of God that leads man to repentance."[28] Even if we fail to understand his true nature, "he remains faithful to his nature, for he cannot deny himself."[29]

But alas! In the absence of such understanding, we yet believe God to have caused our destruction and therefore we miss his saving and rescuing love.

Spiritually speaking man has held to the idea that our lives are blessed or cursed BY GOD, and that, according to how well we behave. This was the thought of the ancient Hebrews who suffered untold miseries, primarily because they "earned it" by missing the mark of God's demands. This has been carried over to every nation, people, and almost every religion on earth, even to this day...even in spite of the truth of God's nature, as defined by Jesus, who brought us the understanding of grace and mercy. Hence we suffer disease, an abomination in the sight of God...wars and personal conflicts, poverty, domestic sadness, gross lack and disappointments. As long as this idea of God prevails, the suffering will continue.

Jesus came along completely turning this thought upside down. And although he promised a better life, proven by his healings and care for the people, they rejected it, and him, for the familiar but death producing old concepts.

No more the divisive horror of the "we, they" doctrine of traditional religion. Never again some separating themselves from others to keep themselves pure. This is the "doctrine of the Nicolaitanes, which thing I hate,"[30] God said. Remember that Jesus loved and "ate with the sinners"[31] to show us the very heart of the Father. No more viewing others as unclean while fancying ourselves pure and the only ones accepted. Such an attitude "strains at a gnat and swallows a camel"[32] of a proud and hardened heart.

He spoke of a new understanding, of a merciful, benevolent God who loved us unconditionally. He told us that there was a Spirit of Life and Truth that would be poured out upon all men everywhere that would "lead and guide us into ALL truth and understanding."[33] He said that the very presence of that Spirit would CAUSE us to know the truth of God and CAUSE us to live life in accordance to his very nature! And out from HIS OWN heart! He said, "All shall know me."[34] Not simply to know about him, but to become intimately acquainted with him, as the word "know" truly means. Grace from his very heart would live within us and by that grace we would be able to receive all the benevolence he had to give and all the understanding we have for centuries longed for. Then he poured out his Spirit, the same Spirit that motivated him and made him who he was, penetrating the hearts and minds of those longing to experience this.

Eternity, by definition, goes both ways. It is existence both before now and after now. It has always been and will always be. The only thing that embraces that definition is an Eternal God. Eternal Life then is Eternal God.

Ephesians declares that we have been in and with this Eternal Life "since before the foundation of the world."[35] Job says that, "The morning stars sang together and the sons of God shouted for joy before ever the world was formed."[36] Psalms 90 tells us this: "Lord you have been our dwelling place in all generations. Before the mountains were brought forth, or ever you formed the earth, even from everlasting to everlasting."[37] Therefore we have been in the experience of Eternal Life forever. The gift of God then is our ability to perceive this. To live out from its very nature.

The manifestation of this Life is realized through the visible creation, primarily man. Eternal Life sought expression and that initiated the visible world. It is the intention of Eternal Wisdom and Infinite Love to express itself through and eventually AS man.

This must be spoken to you by the heart of God. Only the Spirit of truth can reveal this to you. Many are wagging their tongues repeating what they are hearing others say. But it is without power, unable to alter even one error, one disease, one circumstance. This is a walk by revelation and, that, from the heart of God, by way of the gift of the Spirit of truth, all leading us to the fulfillment of HIS purpose...and to the PRESENT experience of Eternal Life.

Revelation comes from the root word reveal. It is

the difference between hearing from man, or hearing a truth that penetrates our heart by the Spirit of Truth, itself. Anything received by revelation is eternally life changing. Once this understanding comes by revelation our hearts are forever changed. We will see this One Life everywhere we look. All of creation will sing of this truth. Wars and conflict will cease. Peace will rule without effort. And it is possible right here, right now!

All this is "light years" away from the awful religious teaching of man born in sin and needing to find a way to please a very disappointed God in order to inherit eternal life! That thought consigns us to a life of self absorption, fear and aloneness. Far away from God, who we then believe is judging and condemning, testing and proving us day by day.

No, my friends. We are sent from God, bearing his Spirit and his Life to fulfill his purpose, which he will cause to happen! We are clean, loved, pure and wonderful in his sight, for he knows there is One Life and we are his.

"He is the true light that lights every man born into the world. And that light IS THE LIFE OF MEN."[38] And that light is you.

CHAPTER FOUR

THE SPIRIT OF LIFE

God breathed the breath of his Spirit of Life into the "nostrils of man" and man began to live. Deep within every man then is Eternal Life. We must awaken to this, by revelation and by experience. Not by simply hearing it taught or reading the ideas of others.

In the Hebrew writings the word "nostril" means "forehead." The forehead is the area in the brain where we feel emotions, make decisions, choose between good or better, motivate our lives, and learn to live within the standards of a sociological structure, among other things. This is the material, anatomical area which enables us to know God. This is where we make our choices and recognize future consequences of behavior or choices of thought. We desire and we love from here. We fear and we hate from here also. This is why the book of Revelation says we will decide to embrace the nature of man (number of man...666) or the nature of God ("You shall receive a new name"[39]...nature) and our choice will be "written on our foreheads"...and lived out in our lives.

This is the heart of the brain so to speak. Here Eternal Life dwells quietly, silently until awakened by the Spirit. Man cannot do this. "For you have not chosen me but I have chosen you."[40] And, "no man comes to the father except he be drawn by the Spirit."[41] So much for the haughty religious tradition that says we choose and therefore are blessed, while others choose not and are eternally cursed.

The gift of Eternal Life is the living of his Life, right here, right now. It is not, as some say, to be delivered with wrapping and bows after you die as a reward for how you have lived. This is very shallow and unsubstantiated by scripture and by revelation.

Early man was instructed to live by partaking of the Wisdom, the understanding, the grace, the Voice of this Life (the fruits of the Tree of Life). He was cautioned not to live by his own intellect, will and cravings, nor to live by his assessments of right and wrong (Tree of (human) knowledge of good or evil)..."For in the day you eat thereof you shall surely die."[42] This is a death to the awareness of Eternal Life. For God is this Life and He is our Life.

Many differences in doctrines have arisen as to how this is to appear...God as our life. But only the Voice of Eternal Life itself can teach you truth in this. And what you choose to receive will be life or death to you. You will choose the age old religious doctrine of human struggle or you will choose the flow of the Eternal Spirit of God living out its Life through you. And that is grace.

Questions will arise. Unchallenged, often mindless teachings of religion and science will need to be met head on, fearlessly challenged. The Spirit of Truth has been freely given. It "will lead and guide you into all truth"[43] and understanding. But you will have to make the firm decision to heed only that Voice. And never be deluded by the "brilliance of man".

Is my life contained within my body? Or is there a Life common to all that easily flows through my mind and body...animating me, living as me? Does the seeming condition of the body determine the future of my life? Is my body my life? Is there such a thing as "my life?" Do I possess it? (see Ezekiel 44:28)

Who really is responsible for this life? Am I? If I were, it would be beneficial to know the future, wouldn't it? Without the future blueprint before me, decisions determining my life, my body, would be difficult, if not impossible.

Is my life predetermined by my genetic code? Or is it eternally intact and indestructible, incorruptible? "For I am your Life and the length of your days."[44] I will experience what I choose here. Am I the result of chance? Or am I the result of a Nature that knows no challenge to it, fears no evil, is never embraced by evil, and never knows death?

Am I the victim of these things, of chance, of genetics, of ancestral sins, of past defeated lives? Or is the substance of my life so eternal, so magnificent, so certain that it roars its presence in the halls of confidence, as a lion roars its kingship and dominance in the jungle?

I, of course, struggled through what I thought was my life, never challenging the nonsense that is insanity to me now. I lived from the certainty that "if it's going to get done, I will have to do it." But when the Spirit of Life awakened in my soul, it began to chip away that foolishness. I learned that to really live was to follow this Voice of Spirit. I thought I had come a long way until an incident happened that would close the door on the ignorance of this once and for all.

BARBARA'S BIRTH

Although I wrote of this in a previous book, I felt to repeat it again here for clarity.

Years ago I was involved in several home births, so when my friend asked that I attend her at her home birth I agreed. Her first two births were hospital births and this time she wanted the intimate, peaceful, family environment. However as the day arrived one of the attending midwives noticed something irregular, a possible breech presentation, and sent her for further evaluation. It was confirmed, Barbara was to have a "butt first" breech baby! At the hospital they warned her of the dire consequences of continuing in the direction she had chosen (home birth), but the only alternative they offered was a caesarian section...which she refused. At home that evening, the labor began. The two midwives busily prepared for the birth, singing and humming and obviously unconcerned about the change of events. I, on the other hand was in a panic. I knew so much. I had seen and studied so much. Horrible things could go wrong which would threaten the very life of the baby. Didn't they know? Didn't they see? Why was I the only one afraid? Was it because they just didn't understand? I sat in a rocking chair and froze. Everyone was waiting for me to make a final decision. The mother and father both wanted the home birth. The midwives wanted the home birth. I thought they were insane! But something held me back. I practically couldn't talk. I just sat there, rocking and barely breathing...and the baby was born. I took her immediately thinking that I was going to need to resuscitate her, but no! She was doing fine! Everyone except me was doing fine!

What happened? What was all that about? I went downstairs and sat in front of the fireplace watching the flames dancing about. I was confused, embarrassed, and beyond frustrated. One of the midwives had been a previous client of mine and came down to join me. She said a few words to me but what I remember from it all was this statement: "You don't trust life. You think you must do it, fix it, make it right. You are afraid to take your hands off it and just trust life to appear in perfect order."

Now, what in the world did that mean? Nothing! I had no idea what she was saying but I knew it was of major importance. Life was what we were all doing. Right? She sounded like it was something that existed independent from us, from me. I drove home slowly. It was 4 a.m. and I was tired and miserable. I fell into my bed at 5 a.m. and was asleep in a second. Twenty minutes later I woke up, wide awake, sitting up in my bed saying out loud, "I get it! There is only One Life, only One Son (manifestation of the Life) and everyone is really IT! That is what we all are! Nothing more, nothing less." The revelation of an eternal, common Life was born in my soul! It has always existed – with or without me (Michele) and therefore eternal and indestructible.

For two years after that I saw and knew nothing else. I was elated beyond any experience this life could offer. Healings happened daily. With no effort. Life was declaring Its glory and Its presence to me! It was announcing, "Here I am. Here I have always been. Everything that exists is ME manifesting myself, declaring my Being. All of creation is ME, visibly expressing myself…all that I am."

Soon the intensity subsided but I would never be the same again. I knew what I knew. I saw what I saw. It is what it is. Whether we know it or not, believe it or not, choose it or not…yet it is what it is.

Life is its own Being. Eternal and forever. Independent and undisturbed by any human ideology, situation or condition. It is who we are and what we are and what will always be. It is what we have come from and who we will always be. It is what formed us and breathed its Spirit into us. It is what Paul spoke of when he said, "The Spirit of Life has made me free from the Law of sin and death."[45] The gift of Eternal Life is awakening to this. Not simply hearing it and agreeing to it. But by entering into the experience of it. And that is the job of the Holy Spirit…the Spirit of Life.

With the dawning of this knowledge and experience we are left with the responsibility of remaining focused and acutely aware of it. At first it feels like something surrounding us, influencing us for good always. Then it becomes apparent that it flows through us and animates us, speaks though us, and thinks through us. As the workings of the Spirit continue it so connects with us in consciousness and heart that it becomes one with us and as us. Now it can be said the "The Father and I are one."[46] This is entirely the workings of the Spirit. Even our desiring this, committing to this, focusing and meditating upon it, as well as its appearing, is all a work of Spirit. We respond. We cooperate. We feel a devotion to this and we realize that it is for this reason we have come. Specifically to allow this Spirit to manifest this Life through each of us. "The earth is filled with the knowledge of the Lord as the waters cover the sea."[47] The reality of this, the visible expression of this can now appear through each of us.

CHAPTER FIVE

MAN'S VIEW OF LIFE
VERSUS
GOD'S VIEW OF LIFE

Man's view of life, humanly speaking, is generally defined by what one does with his life, by what has been achieved along the way. Life is measured by one's education, degrees, letters before or behind one's name...as well as the size of one's bank account, investments, prestigious home and location of that home. We see our life as our own making. We then become personally responsible for it all. This either leads to self exhalation or self recrimination. If personal responsibility becomes too frightening, we decide that God and fate are one and the same, so that whatever happens must have come from God and we had nothing whatsoever to do with it.

Whatever gender we came with also is a major determining factor in our view of, or expectation of, how our life will go, as well as what socio-economic class we were born into. Always looking outside of ourselves for reasons why, we often see ourselves as a product of either the success, or more often, the failure of our parents.

So life, as thus defined by our limited, self absorbed

ideas, begins with birth and ends with death. The arguments are endless about whether life begins at conception, when the heart begins to beat, or at birth. No one is expanding their vision to grasp that life has no beginning nor ending but is in fact an eternal experience. We might think it can be destroyed or interrupted...but this is impossible.

The first chapter of Jeremiah tells us that "before I formed you in the belly I knew you and before you came forth out of the womb I sanctified you...and I ordained you a prophet unto the nations."[48]

"In the beginning was God"[49]...and we were in him...at the beginning. And there really was no beginning! So eternity goes both ways. Both before we arrived here and after we leave here, we find that we too have always been. Safely tucked away, absorbed in Divine Love. Now sent here deliberately and with purpose, that only he who sent us really knows. That makes him, from beginning to end, the only responsible party and we, the humble followers of his Spirit and his Voice.

As an autonomous being, man believes himself to be judged by God continually and always found to be grossly lacking. We pump ourselves up to drown out this horrible sense of inadequacy and failure...perpetual wrongness! We attempt to drown this out by becoming unrelenting judges of others. It's easier to look "out there" at who else is wrong than to look within ourselves. Carrying this idea further we believe then that we will suffer or be blessed forever after we "die" based upon our performance while we are here. We are so entrenched in this doctrine that we interpret the scriptures to reinforce this atrocious idea. One could never accept this once the true nature of God is known.

Does God punish? No, but lest you think I am saying that there is no consequence for sin (error in thinking that results in error of actions)...there is a law of sowing and reaping. Whatsoever we sow that shall we also reap.[50] The law which is being violated does the punishing. Let's say we got all mixed up driving in a new town and found ourselves going the wrong way down a one way street. We were violating a law, whether we knew it or not. If then we found ourselves involved in an accident, did God punish? Or did the law of sowing and reaping (cause and effect) play into effect? If we decide to take a job or marry someone knowing deep in our heart that this is the wrong decision...and it ends in failure, did God cause the failure, or did the law of cause and effect play out to its natural consequence? If you put your hand on a hot stove top and get burned, did God do this or is this the result of what is believed about fire?

How can we escape the ravages of this law? (Which, incidentally, was established to maintain order throughout creation.) The absolute only way to avoid this law of consequences is by either following the Spirit of Life (the Voice of Spirit) in every situation or, if you fail to do this, by humbling oneself as quickly as you can when you realize that you "have run ahead of the Spirit", and then repenting before God. The wonderful news is that act of repentance (just as simple as a Whoops!) will nullify the law of "as you do, so shall you bring back unto yourself."[51] Once the "slate is clean" again, all obstructions to the easy flow of this Life is reestablished, and the Wisdom of the Spirit of Life is leading out once again.

Every transgression is really a violation of the Law of Love. "Love is the fulfillment of the law."(Romans 13:6) If we are perpetually moving in the law of Love, being motivated by a Love so much greater than our own...we cannot transgress the law, (or sin.) Think of it; if you were filled with Love, would anyone need to tell you not to commit adultery? Not to steal? Not to lie about another? Not to gossip or find fault with another? Love is the nature of the Spirit of Life revealed.

There is a scripture that should help here. "The law of the Spirit of Life has made me free from the law of sin (any violation of the law) and death (the penalty for breaking the law)."[52] The Law of the Spirit of Life, (which is living as directed by Love or the Voice of Wisdom) is higher, purer and eternal.

God is Life. The Life of every living thing. To flee from the consequences of living unconsciously (mindlessly going our own way with no regard to Spirit's leading) we must turn to God, the author of Life. Once we realize our mistake, our offense, or transgression and we turn to God with a humble heart, another Law is activated. Immediately. It is the law of grace. Jesus came to teach us grace, ("the law came by Moses, but grace and truth came by Jesus Christ).[53] Grace is the Holy Spirit doing for man what man cannot do without him. Which is EVERYthing!

Grace activates the very heart of God which is Mercy. Enough cannot be said about Mercy. Mercy really is the heart of God. For the hard of heart it is an impossible concept. It actually infuriates people who want others to suffer for offenses. They call that justice. Their god is harsh, punitive and exacting. Impossible to please. But the judgment of God is mercy and not punishment. It is the "goodness of God that causes men to repent."[54] Not punishment. "By mercy and truth iniquity is purged."[55] Not punishment. "Blessed be the man who knows that God does not impute iniquity to his account."[56] The very people who insist on this harsh form of "justice" certainly would not want it for themselves! But alas! They see themselves above offense, so they conclude they can't be hurt by the law of cause and effect. (Which they confuse as God punishing).

But for those of us who know we have offended the law of Love, in words, in thoughts, in actions...we cling to this mercy and find our freedom and release. And we are quick to extend it to others, knowing that to give mercy is to be certain to receive it when the time comes that we need it, which is always.

In the Old Testament the Israelites were instructed to build a huge tent, called The Tabernacle. It was a place to go to worship their God while they marched through the wilderness to their promised land. Deep within the confines of this movable structure was the Presence and Glory of God. It was called the Mercy Seat. This is where they fled to be forgiven of offenses. This was where they turned in times of struggle, conflict, wars, disease, loss or lack. By definition, Mercy is the ability to see beyond the human picture, with all its confusion and apparent failure, and see only the eternal Life of each one of us. This is seeing "not offense" but Life, God, deep within the heart of us all. Once that realization is reached all offenses and their consequences (suffering) are cancelled. Why? Because we have chosen to live in mercy and not in judgment. How great is this Mercy! It cannot be measured! It is the heart and soul of God. And it dwells within each one. The Tabernacle then is the soul of man, while we go deep within our souls to our mercy seat and release the flow of true mercy and forgiveness.

Although the English language uses the word mercy in conjunction with compassion, they are not the same. Once again, mercy is the ability to see beyond the visible conflict to that perfection which never changes. Compassion is most often the activating factor, or catalyst that allows us to experience mercy.

Jesus well spoke when he said, "I will have mercy and not a life of religious sacrifices. Go and learn what that means"![57] For us to show mercy to others is a requirement placed upon us by God, lest we also fail to receive mercy. "Mercy rejoices against judgment."[58] Do we judge another by their sins or mistakes, or do we feel and show mercy instead? Mercy swallows up the demands of the law of do's and don'ts. Just as the Mercy Seat, in the Hebrew Tabernacle, sits high over the Ark of the Covenant which contains the commandments of do's and don'ts.[59] Love or mercy flowing from one's heart will dissolve the need for laws of behavior. It will heal the sinner and restore the sick to wholeness. It is the final law of God.

When you understand that mercy is your freedom

from punishment, and when you choose to deal with others in this same manner, you will be moving in the heart of God. Eternal Life will easily flow to and through you. Everything in your atmosphere of existence will appear in Divine Order. This is what man refers to as healing.

❧

Another widely believed error concerning the nature of God that must be challenged is that God afflicts with evil that good might appear.

Recently a kind gentleman announced that God "blessed him with Parkinson's disease." He accepted this as fact, believing that suffering is God's way of preparing him for heaven hereafter. Isn't it strange that even believing this, folks wiggle and squirm to extricate themselves from the suffering?

To believe that misery is from God, so that the afflicted person will finally serve him, is using pain and fear as an instrument of torture that good might come out of it. What about this idea sounds like "God is Love"? Isn't that the philosophy of Hitler? He would annihilate a race of people so that a more perfect race might appear. We shuddered at his ideology but accept it from God?

God does NOT afflict with evil that good might appear.

It will be impossible to freely, and at any time, receive the abundance of that which is contained in the nature of Eternal Life unless this major error in human thinking is challenged and fully resolved. God does not react. God is always in an acting mode, never reacting. No matter where we have failed, in thought or actions, God does not react to this. God is constant and immutable (unchangeable) love and goodness. This flows to and through us as his Spirit. If we are in error of thoughts or actions...this goodness will correct it. In other words God isn't good to us if we are good, but punishing if we are not so good.

The justice of God is not as the justice of men. The judgment of God is always seen through the eyes of our eternal perfection, as he created us. He sees beyond what we believe we are seeing straight to what he has formed out from his perfection.

It is at this point that well-meaning preachers raise their voices in fear that the unveiling of this truth will give "license to sin." In other words, without punishment what will cause the sinner to want to stop what he or she is doing? But the Scriptures do not say, "where sin abounds, punishment also abounds." No. What it says is that "where sin abounds, GRACE does so much more abound."[60] Grace. That unseen factor freely pouring out from the heart of Love to give us the strength, the desire, the inspiration, to cease from the way we have chosen and choose the way of Love. Grace, Love, Mercy. There is no power so great in all of heaven or earth. No influence so all encompassing. Nothing so effectual to correct and change our course.

God does not withhold. For any reason. No more than the sun could cease to shine. God cannot deny his own nature. We may have not yet opened our hearts to receive, but what God gives is always being poured out to us. If we stand in the shade we cannot feel the effects of the sun. But the sun is still shining.

So once again, "the rain falls on the just and the unjust alike. The sun shines on the good and the unthankful."[61] This is probably one of the most startling words of truth ever spoken. It rips away our self righteous ideas that hold God accountable to punish and destroy those who fall under the influence of evil. "He does not deal with us according to our iniquities."[62] And he charges us not to do so to others either!

Looking once again at the scripture, "by mercy and truth iniquity is purged."[63] Retribution and punishment only serve to increase the sense of condemnation and failure in the heart of the sinner. This then is the power which tightens the grip of darkness that surrounds us. "The strength of sin (disease and death) is condemnation."[64] Why would God then (even if he could) do something that would cause us to continue in failure and suffering?

From this place of Infinite Mercy the blazing, all encompassing Glory of God bursts forth with forgiveness, healing and provisions. All that man could ever need. Paul, in the book of Hebrews instructs us to "come boldly to this throne of mercy that we may find the grace and help we need for any situation,"[65] declaring that this structure yet remains deep in the soul of every man...waiting for us to reach for it, to touch it, to find it for every need.

When we experience mercy and goodness...and we know we have not by our behavior, earned it...it begins to soften us. Then the covering, the blinding veil which has held us in bondage begins to loosen its grip on us.

Remember that we must always "make the separation" between the individual and the offensive behavior or disease...that which is clearly come to "steal, kill, and destroy."[66] Just because something is manifesting through one's life, or mind, or body, doesn't mean that it has originated there.

Any reference to God's wrath against evil in the Sacred Scriptures is actually the goodness of God removing from us whatever is attempting to destroy us. God's "wrath" is against anything that appears to hurt us, never against us. We see in nature the maternal wrath of a lion, a bear, a wolf and really almost any animal whose offspring is being threatened. So when we are threatened with evil of any appearance, the maternal wrath of God will, with vengeance, come to destroy it and protect us against any harm. "Surely goodness and mercy shall follow me all the days of my life. And I will dwell in the house (heart) of God forever."[67] God always makes the separation between us and that which is come to destroy.

"He is the true Light, which lighteth every man that cometh into the world. And that Light is the LIFE of man."[68] Therefore, man is the Light and Life of God. That is an eternal truism and cannot be changed. Ecclesiastes, Chapter 7, says that God made man to reign superior to the challenges of darkness but "man has sought out many evil imaginations."[69] Many false beliefs have reduced man to what we see today. Man has ignorantly allowed multiple coverings of thought, doctrine and beliefs to hide that light. But through it all the penetrating voice of Jesus rings throughout eternity, "You are the Light of the world. Don't let it be hid under a bushel (false covering)."[70]

We must awaken to the realization that we cannot be sick or evil, confused or lost. We are the image of Divine Order and it is the Spirit of Life that blazes through us that keeps us intact forever in that state.

"Each seed reproduces after its own kind."[71] We are forever in the image of what has created us and brought us forth.

What afflicts us is not a particular disease or sinful nature, but the dull, stuporous condition of thought that believes we can be sick or believes we can behave badly. Then any imagination of evil can appear.

Once the mercy of God has awakened us we will choose the truth and turn and walk away from the whole miserable scenario, the whole sordid scene before us.

Now what if, for all the goodness bestowed upon us, for all the truth set before us, we yet continue in our present darkness? This is where the law of sowing and reaping, cause and effect, will actually work for us. We will reap the effects of what we are holding onto. It will inadvertently cause destruction in our lives because it is an interruption in the Divine Order that God has established...that we always move in love and in obedience to the Spirit that governs us. When suffering, pain and sorrow appear, that will turn us to the light of truth, seeking deliverance and the mercy that will free us. This is unfortunately interpreted as God causing the suffering.

But he is not. It is instead the logical consequence of what we have set in motion. It is the consequence of holding onto a snake that we would be bitten. Divine Mercy stands by to immediately deliver the moment you realize what you are doing and choose to take hold of his grace and turn away from whatever ideas or beliefs that led to your suffering.

The belief in human conflict will continue to appear as anger, hate, lawsuits, divorce, holding grudges and wars until we wake up and realize that God is Love and God is One. We are actually turning against our own life, cannibalizing our own souls to our own destruction. Eventually we will repent, turn to the truth that there really is only One Begotten Son (one common Life) and receive the flow of the Eternal Life once again.

The belief that weather conditions are the result of random wind activity and the like, and that we are at the mercy of such, will continue until we remember that God rules in Order and in Love and "never sleeps or slumbers." [72] To live under such a sense of separation from his continual care is to invite such experiences, and then call it an "act of God." Oh, the ignorance of the wisdom of men!

Through it all the triumphant shout from heaven is heard that "all shall know me from the least to the greatest."[73] And "every knee shall bow and every tongue confess."[74] "He is the true light that lighteth every man born into the world and his light is the Life of men."[75] This Life is strong, eternal and well able to reveal itself as uninterruptable Divine Order.

"It is finished. It is done." We need only to receive it with a thankful heart to experience it.

So if suffering is not God's way for good to appear, what is God's way? It is the office of the Holy Spirit freely given to all men everywhere that deals in the hearts of men, to cause the goodness that is God to begin to arise from the depths of every person. It is the purpose and intention of God to reveal himself through his creation and the way to do this is the activity of the Spirit. We must learn to trust the Spirit will do what it was sent to do. We must begin to look at it long and hard and finally come to grips that it does not need us to suffer or to help it along. Only to respond to its Presence.

When Mary was told by the angel Gabriel that she would birth the son of God she said, "How can this be?"[76] There was no human way possible. The same is true of us. There is no human way possible for us to bring forth the fullness of God, and human effort is surely inadequate to even try. Only the Holy Spirit can cause this to appear through you and me. Just as the angel told Mary that "the Holy Spirit would overshadow her and the power of the highest would be upon her to bring this forth."[77] So it is with you and me.

No suffering necessary. No human works to achieve necessary. Just trusting this Spirit to fulfill its eternal mission.

Chapter Six

UNDERSTANDING THE IDEA
OF COVERINGS
"MAKING THE SEPARATION"

What is a "covering?" It is anything that governs us, any idea or philosophy of belief that we subscribe to. Any power, real or imagined, that seems to have power to bless or curse us. A covering can be very benign, harmless, even very good for us, like a loving parent, a benevolent God, an honest non-corrupted community or national government. Or a covering can be malignant, obtrusive, vicious and deadly, such as the widespread belief that disease has power, that God ordained suffering to punish us, that we must be good in order to please God and get to heaven, or a corrupted, self serving government, abusive parents, domestic violence and the like.

The Bible refers to coverings as garments also. One can be covered by the light of truth or the darkness of fear. One can wear the garment of trust and joy or the garment of self preservation, self serving, self responsibility, selfishness. One can thrive under the covering of pure joy for another's good fortune or turn inside out with jealousy, anger, and covetousness.

We can choose to take off these ideological garments and replace them with another any time we choose. We are not usually forced to live under a certain covering...we can choose another and invite and allow the Spirit within us to occupy that space and correct whatever we have allowed to cover us. Just as soon as we realize the presence of the Spirit occupying that space the covering is automatically corrected. We don't do it. We simply allow the Spirit to fill the space previously occupied by the false ideology or abusive presence.

The covering is not who we are. We are still the same under it. It cannot change our basic nature made in the light of God with his Eternal Life as our Eternal Life. But it can alter our experience here for good or evil. Since it is not who we are we can walk away from one and put on another and change our experience. It comes down to we being the one choosing to determine our present environment (bodies included) or our choosing to live in reaction to whatever is appearing.

How can anything truly made from the perfection of an eternal God fall into confusion, chaos and darkness? Doesn't "each seed reproduce after its own kind?"[78] Do we not possess the "mind of Christ?"[79] If so, how can we think thoughts of hate, condemnation and judgment? Is the Divine Life that formed us and sent us here really the whole substance of our being? Then how can the life that we truly are suffer disease? Is the nature of God love, goodness and mercy? Doesn't that make it our nature as well? How is it that we can put ourselves first before another, devise ways to "get more," live to gain instead of living to give?

What causes the contradictions we see and struggle against?

The most insidious and malignant doctrine that has covered mankind, the most death producing, causing man to end in destruction is the idea of "original sin." It starts us out in destruction and failure and insures that we will stay that way. When the premise is wrong the conclusion will of course be wrong. No matter what we do according to the myriad of religious practices to climb out from under that image, we still carry the weight of it throughout our lives. It keeps us in a perpetual state of condemnation and unworthiness, which is the foundation of all disease.

Dealing a death blow to the holy words of God, himself, we say, "We were not really made in the image of God but in disgrace and sin, worthy to suffer, always to fail. Needing to experience pain and anguish to purge us of this awful condition." Tell me, have you ever known anyone in the throws of deep suffering that has felt free from the sense of failure and unworthiness? Don't you know that it only deeply intensifies their sense of being a miserable sinner, now punished for their terrible failures. I have often said in the past fifty years of caring for sick folks that I should have a dollar for everyone who has looked up at me from their bed of horror and asked me, "What did I ever do to deserve this?" Feeling judged and a failure is always one basis for us unconsciously accepting suffering and disease in our lives.

Hence we accept disease and pain, sorrow and

defeat and believe it is "God's will" that we do so! Until and unless we choose to go against the current flow of popular thought and religious nonsense, and begin to believe the words, "man was made in the image and likeness of God,"[80] we will forever doom ourselves to pain and suffering, conflict and defeat.

How could anything that has come forth from God, made in the likeness of God, ever fall into corruption? The answer to that question is...it can't really...only in our imagination but never in reality.

When do we get to see this in the human picture? Just as soon as we realize that the Spirit has forever been flowing through us all along and giving us the faith (the realization) to accept it. Remember that we "live by faith and not by sight." First we choose to accept this in spite of what we are seeing and then we are able to actually begin to feel it. How does this happen? The same way we accepted the "great lie." We were programmed. Now we are reprogramming our conscious awareness with truth and "out from this comes the issues of life."[81] Disease, wars and human sorrow will then be seen to be an unfortunate hysterical insanity. But until we cross this line and choose to stay there, we will continue to experience such destruction.

Either, "all the works of his hands are perfect,"[82] and "we are his masterpiece creation in perfection,"[83] or we come stained, corrupted and designed to fail. Either, "he is our life,"[84] and therefore we share a common life, an eternal life, or there is no hope.

One idea honors our Creator and one dishonors

him. We must choose.

This original sin idea began in Genesis, chapter 2, and from then on, book by book in the Bible we see mankind struggling under this awful believed identity. All the way through we read of promises from God that this will end and we will finally experience who we are and why we are here. But the years have come and gone and man is weary of waiting. Soon all hope of this appearing here on earth vanished and man created then a new doctrine or covering. One that declares that we must wait until we die to see it and it is up to us to earn it. This is a vicious covering that has produced a deep sense of failure and unworthiness to receive anything from God. I have found this basic covering so deeply embedded in the hearts of mankind to be the absolute reason we cannot receive from our beloved Creator who shines his goodness upon all of his creation, always. What is the answer to this? How will we come out from under this? How can we possibly take on the same deep conviction of our true being and identity? The answer lies with the Holy Spirit of Eternal Life...for this is his whole intention and activity.

We hear so much lately about "watching our thoughts." But I want to advance the idea that those thoughts we are trying not to entertain are not our thoughts at all! "Can both bitter and sweet waters come forth from the same fountain?"[85] No, they cannot. Only the Divine Mind exists and that is our mind. With it we cannot think anything evil or confused or convoluted at all. Only pure reflections of the beauty of this eternal Life we live in and which lives in us can come forth from our minds. That makes all thoughts that are unlike this simply a covering coming from the mass confusion and hysteria of the prevailing human consciousness.

But we came here with a mission. We were deliberately sent to this atmosphere of thought (earth) to bring light, Life, truth, peace and harmony to an atmosphere described as being "without form and void."[86] This means the space was empty...with darkness covering...resulting in chaos, confusion and disorientation swirling about, (mass consciousness). It was in need of order, the light of understanding, harmony and peace, and the knowledge of pure goodness ruling and reigning. And when the Creative Good declared that there must be light in this place,[87] you arrived...the Light of the world.[88]

We brought with us, and in us, all that would ever be needed to subdue and take dominion over such confusion. We brought heaven. So that "as in heaven it would also be on earth."[89] This atmosphere of confusion contains all the conflicting thoughts and ideas you have been led to believe come from you. But now we know that this is not possible. Now we know we are not thinking them but hearing them. Now we can hold out our hand and say, "No!"

This "void and darkness," this insidious belief that we come stained with sin and corruption, is actually the "veil spread over all nations."[90] It is a covering of darkness, devoid of understanding, without the light of truth. Once the veil or covering is removed, all the confusion naturally clears up. All the pain and sorrow it caused would disappear. All the fears and madness would be gone. All the insane thoughts we now entertain would disappear.

This veil, this thick covering is, you see, only the absence of light, of truth, of understanding. Darkness is not an entity of its own. It is the absence of light. Cold is not an entity of its own. It is the absence of heat. A space that is empty is not an entity...it is merely a space waiting to be filled. When true substance (truth) appears the space ceases to be a space at all. Now it is filled. "The truth makes us free!"[91]

We come bearing the nature of him who sent us. This is both our substance and our covering. This is the meaning of the Genesis story of the firmament divided above and beneath with dry land appearing between.[92] Our present mortal experience here is dry land. Heaven is both within and without us. It is covering us, acting as a garment of light and wisdom. It is also deep within us, awakening us to the amazing truth of who we are, where we have come from and the power given to us to accomplish what we have been sent to do.

There is a pre-established Divine Order for both heaven and earth. It is maintained and sustained by the Holy Spirit, as we choose to yield to it. This is our guide, our counselor, our wisdom, our teacher, our great comforter. This is the Divine Presence that informs us that we actually are the Son of God, all as one and one as all. It is what enables us to actually grasp and utilize this truth.

The children of Israel wandered for forty years in the wilderness marching to the fulfillment of their promise but died in the wilderness "having never received the promise."[93] Because they thought it depended on them even though they knew they couldn't do it. Instead of trusting the workings and intention of God, as well as the very purpose of the indwelling Spirit of God to bring forth "after its own kind,"[94] they threw up their hands in despair and wandered until they all died.

When we choose this Spirit of Eternal Life as our covering, day in and day out, we are able to both live well and fulfill the intention of God who sent us here…to be the light of understanding, filling the void and dissolving the ignorance and blindness of false coverings.

Grace is the whole answer. This is the activity of the Holy Spirit in and through us which causes paradise to reappear. Over and over it must be stated until by deep reflection it is actually felt, "I will pour my Spirit out upon all flesh and by my Spirit you shall know me, understand me, follow my leadings, from the least to the greatest. All shall partake of this. I will not ever look at your failures but only at the fulfillment of my word."[95] From beginning to end grace is the whole answer. Jesus said that to receive anything spiritually we must first "believe we have already received and we shall then experience it."[96] We must now pause and allow ourselves the moment to feel the covering of this Spirit. We must allow it access to every aspect of our lives and body. This is the beginning of taking on the new covering and ultimately the true identity that we have come to experience.

Spiritually in the heavens the order is clear. God is the Supreme Being. The Son (visible manifestation of the father) is under the covering of God, the Source. And we, the offspring (the Son) are under the covering of the Spirit being prepared to mature into the full manifestation of the Son.

"All creation groans and travails together in pain waiting for the manifestation of the sons of God."[97] So from this we see that creation falls under our covering. As we flounder about still believing in suffering, in disease, in conflict, pain and lack, so does creation suffer under this consciousness, this covering. But the day is upon us when we rise up to the authority designed for us and put all that confusion under our feet. Then will creation sing and rejoice for their long night will be over as well.

Dis-ease is a false covering, primarily the result of conflict, anxiety, unrest, uncertainty...which will always appear when we fall under the ideology of generations of religious voices telling us we are responsible to do something (or to suffer) to gain the fulfillment of happiness and heaven. It tells us that we must "do it" but then tells us that we cannot achieve this. "All your attempts at righteousness is as a filthy rag."[98] And again, "When you have done all you still must say that you are yet an unprofitable servant."[99]

Dis-ease begins with disease of the mind, false ideas and beliefs we come under, and is then reflected on the body. Our children come under our beliefs as long as they are children. We are their immediate covering. When I receive a call for help concerning a child my focus is always to clear the covering...the tenacious and fearful thoughts of the seriousness of the child's sickness...that rests upon the parents, or adults caring for them.

Human, mortal coverings are full of ideas generated by man's feeble attempt at wisdom without yielding to the Divine Mind. Mortal coverings of thoughts, beliefs, ideologies and philosophies that men live under are imaginations (see Ecclesiastes 7:29) that occupy space until the true substance of understanding fills it. So in the absence of a heart immersed in Divine Love, imaginations of conflict, hate, greed, judgments, criticalness and the like occupy the atmosphere. In the absence of the true realization of abundant provision, imaginations of lack, loss, personal sense of responsibility with the resultant stress, conflicts, fear of failure and uncertainty fills the void we have been sent to. With the inability to "see" or perceive the paradise that surrounds us always, man will take on the very coverings he was sent to replace! We either yield to earth's coverings by the multitude of human reactions or we yield to the garment, the covering of heaven...the Infinite Wisdom of the One Mind.

Hence the parable of the man who came to the wedding feast without a wedding garment.[100] Eternal union with our Divine Source (wedding) can only be accomplished as we come under and yield to the covering of his nature. And so it is called the marriage feast of the Lamb,[101] signifying that only as we yield to the nature of the lamb can we enter into this state of being. That is humility, servant-hood, submission and obedience, and absolute trust in the guidance of the Shepherd of our soul. "And they followed the Lamb withersoever he goeth."[102]

To understand this idea of coverings more fully we might look at the human family unit designed by God. Family works best when the father has as his covering the Holy Spirit, leading him in wisdom and stability. The mother then can trust herself and her children to live protected under the covering of the father. The children thrive under the loving covering of a very peaceful and contented mother. With the divorce rate amazingly high we might look at the failure of this scenario. When this structure is fractured confusion reigns and the consequences are astonishing. (This is not always the conclusion for single mothers or fathers but just an example.)

Proverbs says where the sluggard rules the city the people mourn, but where the prince rules the city the people rejoice.[103] Here it is speaking of the government of our own souls (the city). We must choose how we will govern our lives, our hearts, what we chose to believe and yield to...under the faithful covering of the Spirit of Divine Wisdom or again in reactions to our environment.

Other false coverings are feeling separated, isolated, attempting to climb and scratch our way through this life "the best we can." A very prevalent false covering now is "I am the designer of my own life. I do what I want, as I want. I come under no other authority but what pleases me. I make my own rules and I break them as I please. I am my own authority." And we easily see the confusion this ideology has caused our society and family structure.

In John, chapter 9, Jesus met a blind beggar along the way who cried out for healing. He had been blind since birth. This man is symbolic of us all. The way Jesus healed him was to make clay and cover his eyes. This signified that the "human condition" (clay) was what blinded him. He was covered by the ideology of human thoughts and beliefs. Blinded by the concept of mortality and its subsequent victimhood. Jesus then instructed him to, "Go wash in the pool called, 'To be Sent.'"[104] Which he did. When he washed away the clay (human blindness,) he was able to "see" that he was not the poor fragile victim that he believed himself to be, but was actually a Divine being, immutable and incorruptible, sent here for a very specific purpose and intention. To be fulfilled by the Spirit. ("For this mortal must put on immortality and this corruptible must put on incorruption")[105] He awakened to his true covering. His eyes were opened.

Here is the truth. We don't need to change anything. We are as we have been created, formed and sent. We only need the blinding veil of human thinking to be removed. We need to remember and accept once again who we are and why we are.

There is that which cannot sin. "That which is born of God cannot sin."[106] Only that which is covered and yielding to strange ideologies can sin. You cannot think a thought that does not come from Divine Mind, for there is only One Mind and it is your mind. But you can yield to thoughts that come from evil imaginations that swirl around and about your head. This is our choice.

We cannot fall apart or break down. But we can yield to such ideas of darkness and confusion.

We cannot deal in any way short of Love. But we can respond to the ceaseless promptings of the thick darkness of human imaginations and darkened understandings.

Never again believe that a negative thought can proceed from your mind.

Now what is the advantage of this knowledge? The simplicity of sending away a negative thought much as you would wave away a bothersome fly...as opposed to "owning" the thought and then wondering how to extricate yourself from it. Feeling condemned for thinking it. Feeling worthy of the suffering you are experiencing. Thinking the thought came from you and therefore defines you.

When you see another under any covering of destruction, do you condemn him? Do you think it is who he is? Do you not see a holy son of God trapped under a web of confusion, a false covering? Do you know that your mercy will deliver him but your judgment will condemn him...and you?

When I was in Bible school in my twenties there was a twenty-five year old girl who was raised in a mental institution because she was born there and no one knew what else to do with her. This was before child protective services began. She was pathetically insane. She babbled all the day long and made no sense at all. Sometimes she would become aggressive and violent and would need to be restrained. It was during those times that I learned the power of seeing beyond the covering.

The elders of the school decided to set up a twenty-four hour prayer vigil for her. She was strapped to a bed, screaming and babbling, had not eaten or drunk for days. Had not slept or stopped talking for days. I wanted to help so I signed up for two hours in the middle of the night while my children slept and a teenage girl could stay with them.

I was so moved by her plight that I spent hours praying that day to really be able to help her. Sometime that afternoon a friend of mine shared a dream she had of this girl. She saw her as a very tiny person down in the bottom of a large, empty oil drum banging on the sides of the drum, crying and begging for someone to hear her and let her out. But everyone just passed by and no one heard. When she told me her dream I began to cry. I knew then that what I was seeing was not who she was at all. For the first time in my life I saw that people all too often think the behavior is who they are and so feel trapped, scared, defeated and all alone. For the first time I was able to distinguish between the person and the behavior or the disease.

When my time came, I entered the room a different person than I had ever been. I was so full of compassion and so full of a boldness and strength...the others looked at me like I was some stranger. Right away I knelt down next to her ear and began to talk to the girl inside the oil drum. I told her I heard her cries and that I would never leave her until she was free. She was not alone. Suddenly she got louder and louder, screaming and spitting and swearing. But I didn't care. It was not her. I began to sing in her ear a song of God's unfailing love for her. She was crazy with fury. Soon the others in the room began to sing also. And finally in about an hour it broke and she fell asleep. She slept for two days and woke up in her right mind for the first time in her life.

I would never be the same again. I would never look at a person with a disease and think it was them. I would never look at a defeated, broken man and think it was who he was. I would never look at a half dressed, overly made up female, acting out a part of her pretend world and think that was her. I would see beyond the false coverings. I would see who they were. That which never changed. And I would know I could call it forth and it would come forth.

Coverings are also thoughts of others. Many folks I work with are really struggling, trying to stay on the right track with their thoughts and holding to the truth. They are remembering that they are filled with the Spirit, that it is their only substance. Many are fighting for their lives. But they often feel a heaviness at home knowing the fears and doubts and concerns of their families. This acts as a weight of great proportions. Some never can transcend the coverings placed upon them by their loved ones. Even when not a word is spoken. Most calls I receive are people concerned about a family member who is ill or "off track" somehow. They have no idea how their thoughts and worries keep the problem perpetuated and add to the anguish of another. I always talk to them about their thoughts and how they are seeing through the eyes of darkness if they agree with the problem and then worry about it. I tell them the healing cannot come until they repent for what they are seeing and choose to know and declare the truth about the one they are so concerned about. They must do this and hold to it. Such is the burden of the healer. Such is the burden of the one who loves. Often they say to me that in doing so, it feels as though they stopped caring altogether. This is because we equate love with fretting and worrying. But this is not love at all. The greatest demonstration of love is one who prays to know and see pure truth in everyone. Such will bring to appearance the kingdom of God...here on earth.

This is the value of understanding the concept of coverings. This is the only way we can fulfill our divine purpose. This is how we heal and this is the confidence we need to do it.

The book of Revelation is the ultimate writing concerning the idea of coverings.

First I must say that this book is not to be feared as most folks often say to me. This is the book, more than any in the Bible, which is actually our hope and the reason for our hope. It was never meant to be understood by the natural mind. It was never meant to be interpreted by man. It was certainly not to be revealed to anyone who yet insisted on a God of wrath and fierce judgment. Until God is known deep in your heart as pure love only, you will not be able to read this without getting the whole thing wrong.

Revelation is exactly what it describes itself to be...the revealing of Jesus Christ. This is the true "coming" or reappearing of the promised son to the earth...and it is coming through you and me. This is a book about us. Not nations "outside of us" warring with one another but a description of the internal conflict within each one as we strive to know Him, and to release him from the depths of our souls to be revealed through us and then to a waiting world.

What is the goal here? Why do we pursue the knowledge of God? Is it out of fear of punishment? I hope we have done away with that death-dealing, vindictive ideology by now. Why do those of us who spend our lives, our efforts and our dreams reaching for understanding do it?

I believe there is a Spirit deep within us who, like the seed planted in the ground, strives to be released. It is ITS NATURE to flow and express itself and in order to do this it must find an avenue of release. It awakens at different times throughout our eternal journey, obviously depending on the purposes of Divine Intelligence. In 1 Corinthians, chapter 15, we read that there are many differing "bodies" and species and each one moves individually in response to the promptings of the Spirit...including you and I. We think that the constant stirring within that prompts us along is coming from us...but it is not. "No man comes to the Father unless he is drawn by the Spirit."[107] It is no mystery. It is simply "our time" for Jesus Christ, the "fullness of the manifested Father" to be revealed through us.

Revelation is a book that describes in allegories and symbolisms the methodical removal of the layers of coverings (seals) over us, by the way of false ideologies and perceptions that block his appearing. And for this we must be very grateful. Finally the hope of the whole earth is being revealed. In the words of a dear friend of mine, "Nobody dies!" All that is destroyed is what has for generations been destroying us. There is no wrath against us! The wrath is against what has blinded and hurt us...much like the wrath of the maternal nature in all of creation as she protects her young.

If we knew this, we would hide ourselves away deep under the shadow of the Almighty, until the "indignation be overpast."[108] When we feel turmoil in our lives, souls, we must stop looking at what seemed to cause it and realize that yet another covering is being removed and when the darkness of the night is far spent, joy will come in the morning.[109] Haven't we seen that at the end of every conflict we feel deeper and much more stable spiritually than we did prior to the onset? Look at the death of Jesus, when three days later he awakened to a dimension of existence far above where he was during his earthly ministry. Every "death" is but the removal of a covering, needful for a new and glorious appearing of the Spirit of Life from deep within us.

The "throne room"[110] spoken of throughout Revelation is the Seat of Source, out from where all of life flows. As we experience these coverings being removed we find we can access this place of power and authority over all circumstances much more freely. The end result is that the fullness of God is fully revealed and God is seen to be all in all.[111]

When we understand this working of the Spirit we can cooperate with it better and actually not dread the process at all. It is only when we resist it through lack of understanding and fear that we experience suffering. "Hid in Christ in God"[112] is our place of safety. True understanding is what enables us to find that place of safety as the sprout of Eternal Life comes working its way up through the layers of earth bound thought unto the light of day, showing its blazing glory and eternal nature. Becoming one hundred thousand times greater than when it was just a seed tucked away deep in our souls awaiting its day of glory.

CHAPTER SEVEN

THERE IS NO OPPOSING POWER

Jacob was a twin, the second to appear to his father, Isaac and his mother, Rebecca. The name of his brother who birthed first was Esau. It is said that Esau was a hunter, a man of the earth, while Jacob was a shepherd, more of a dreamer. This is significant as we are told that the first nature to appear (in the soul of man) is a result of the earth born consciousness (Adam). It is "programmed" for conflict and problems. It assumes either the role of a victim or an aggressor. It is "of the earth, earthy."[113] The second nature to appear is the heaven born understanding, the Christ of God. The first must diminish for the second to bloom in its full potential.

One night Jacob had a dream.[114] He dreamt of a ladder reaching from earth to heaven with angels ascending and descending. This is a significant message from Spirit to us "who have ears to hear."[115] It tells us that there are progressive levels of understanding which we must embrace to reach the full acceptance and experience of God occupying all and in all. It is said that angels minister truths to us. Each truth causes us to ascend higher in our spiritual experience. It is well to note that in order to climb a ladder, we must let go of what we stood on previously to take hold of the new rung. We are grateful for what was embraced earlier but now are ready to "see things differently.

One of these new rungs on the ladder is revealed here:

To the Hebrews evil came from "the wrath of God." Jesus, willing to "meet them where they were" spoke of an entity he referred to as a devil. (A conjunction of do-evil). This at least caused them to stop blaming God (pure Love and goodness, forgiveness and mercy) for their calamities. It was a step up the ladder. He showed them the power they had over d-evil. Again and again he proved his power over this d-evil and told them they also had such power.

This was the precursor to the next rung of the ladder...removing from mankind entirely the idea of conflicting good and evil into the realization of absolutely One Life...known as the Tree of Life, in the midst of the paradise of God.[116] Leading us to the eventual understanding that there is no evil in a creation filled with the Presence of God...Omnipotent. Once that is deeply embraced and "felt" in one's heart, evil will certainly cease to appear.

Jesus said there were many things yet that he wanted to share with his disciples but he knew they were, at that level, unable to embrace them. He said instead that he would "send the Spirit of truth to lead and guide them into ALL truth."[117] So we have the idea here that there will be more truth to learn. Now finally we are at the place where we must let go of what can no longer serve us and open ourselves to this Spirit. If we cling to the old for safety and security, we miss what we came to learn and experience...and eventually become.

Paul taught in 1 Corinthians 14 of the many "gifts" of the Spirit. And yet he also told of the time to come when these gifts should "cease," making way for the fullness of "Love" to appear.

Isaiah, chapter 46, instructs us that we "must remember not the former things, neither consider the things of old" so that God may "do a new thing" in the earth.

So now we know that evil is not an entity, not even a power at all. It has no creator, no substance, no life, and there are no adhesive or cohesive properties to it. In the words of Mary Baker Eddy, it is "nothing calling itself something." It is nothing more than evil imaginations. The fear we bring to it is its only power. Take away the fear, or any reaction to it, and the power to harm, to steal, kill and destroy is gone. In the Genesis, Chapter 3, allegory we have the serpent talking to Eve. The Hebrew word for serpent here is fear. And fear is dissolved when pure understanding of the unchangeable nature and intentions of God are embraced with love and hearts full of appreciation. This is miles above the empty parroting of truths, with hopes that that will somehow cause changes in the human picture to appear. This is speaking of hearts full of love for both the truth and the One who brought them to our awareness.

John tells us the truth alone is impotent without the Spirit. "These two must agree,"[118] he says. Truth and

Spirit are married and cannot be divided. It is the heartfelt devotion and immeasurable Love that Spirit births in our soul. It is the sheer inexpressible delight that comes when we remember that we live right now in the kingdom of God, where there can only be harmony, peace, and fulfillment. This is the factor that moves the mountains that arise before us.

Looking at the entirety of creation, from the vantage point of the Creator, we learn that the Spirit of Eternal Life, out from whom all things have appeared, sees only what he has formed by his creative Word and that, exactly as he imaged it to appear, eternal, pure and perfect. Beautiful beyond words to express. To God, who is only good, who declares "that the works of his hands are perfect", there is no evil. There is nothing except pure Life because nothing can proceed from God that is unlike God. "Each seed reproduces after its own kind."[119] A carrot must bring forth a carrot. An acorn must bring forth an oak tree. A bird cannot bring forth an insect. An elephant cannot bring forth a kangaroo. God cannot bring forth evil. Nor can he bring forth anything that can be so unstable and changeable as to become evil. Unlike religious parroting that has gone on for centuries, God did not create a man that could rebel against his Creator, or against his own nature. Why do we see man rebelling so? Because we cling to the evil imagination that we can. When we choose to let go of that concept and embrace the truth of man created in the image of God...this then shall appear. "The earth is the Lord's and everything within it.[120] "We are his masterpiece, created in perfection."[121] Indeed the final act in this human scenario is that God, pure and crystal clear will be seen to be "all and in all."[122]

How do we reconcile this unchallengeable, obvious truth with what we see? We begin by accepting that God's viewpoint is correct, and it is we who are mistaken. "Let God be true and every man a liar."[123] Humans, perceiving life upside down and backwards, will only see lack, loss, grief, despair, and continual wanting. And from this unreal perception myriads of evil images will appear.

Ecclesiastes, Chapter 7, gives us the clearest understanding of this dilemma. "God created man to walk upright (as a prince in glory and majesty)...but man has sought out many evil imaginations."[124] So this is our only enemy. Evil imaginations that deny the nature of God, that deny the truth of God, and that deny the works of God. Evil imaginations that claim their birthright because of the lack of understanding of truth. No small wonder that Proverbs tells us over and over again "in all thy getting, get wisdom and get understanding."[125] Not from men but directly from the Spirit of Truth given to us to "lead and guide us into all truth."[126] We are to "drink water out of the well from our own cisterns, and not another's."[127]

This then is the beginning of what Jesus referred to as the "doctrines of men"[128] which have held us in darkness, suffering, and confusion for centuries. To understand this we must begin by realizing what evil really is and is not. Before we do this it is well to remember that we were severely charged NOT to partake of the knowledge of evil versus good, "for in the day you do thereof, you shall surely die."[129] And die we have been doing ever since! It is long overdue that we look at this "wonder" that has held mankind captive for so long, once and for all, that we might understand, turn, and with the greatest of confidence, simply walk away from it all..

Many who read this are suffering in the most intense circumstances in their lives right now. These words are not to minimize your agony but to deliver you from it. This is not to be insensitive but to destroy what has come to destroy you, "that you might have Life and that more abundantly."[130]

Evil is not a real entity! It is any place in one's consciousness where Eternal Life has not revealed itself to us. It is a VOID. An empty room, dark and unoccupied by any awakened awareness of the blazing Glory of Life realized. This is the understanding of the words, "The earth (you) was without form and void and darkness (lack of understanding) covered the face of the deep."[131]

Since it is a space not visibly filled with Life, it is therefore capable of being filled by whatever is believed on the horizon of man's thinking, whatever is occupying the current atmosphere of human thinking. Words of truth alone will never fill that space. Deep penetrating reflection on any truth until it is felt is required. The delight and joy that always follows will fill that space. Then out from the midst of your being the human condition will be corrected.

There was a time in ancient Hawaii where the inhabitants knew nothing of disease. Until missionaries landed and brought their diseases...actually they brought their beliefs in human failure and in evil. Until then the

Hawaiians only knew freedom, joy and delight. They had no knowledge of disease and therefore were fearless of what they knew nothing about. Now into the void came...the knowledge of evil, sin, fear, defeat, punishment and disease. It is documented that thousands of Hawaiians died on the beaches of measles and syphilis, after that consciousness was presented to them.

"The earth was without form and void and darkness covered the face of the deep." The problem is what we put into the void. When we clearly see and feel the "earth filled with the Glory of God as the waters cover the sea"[132]...and when there is no place, nor space, not filled with his Presence and goodness and freedom to live and love and laugh...then there will be no void to be filled with ideas of ignorance and judgment and fear.

The only solution to the problem of evil is to gain a new and eternal perspective on it. One that enables us to live above such manifestations and one that never dishonors the nature of God.

God said to the Israelites, "Come. Let us reason together."[133]

If God is the only power...then there is no opposing factor.

If God is the only Presence...then there is no opposing factor.

If there is only One Life...then there is no opposing factor.

If evil is not a part of the Divine nature and God is the only Creator...then there is no opposing factor.

If God holds his creation in the palm of his hand,

safe and secure under the shadow of the Almighty..."and no one shall ever be able to pluck them out of my hand"[134]...then there is no opposing factor.

Evil is a term given to any evidence of confusion, chaos, the absence of good...of life...of harmony...of Divine Order. Truly we live in the kingdom of perpetual goodness where no opposing factor exists. Can we delight in the knowledge of this? If so, we can see eminent change coming.

The belief in the presence of evil is a denial of God as filling all space...Omnipresence.

It is a denial of Spirit as directing all the issues of life.

It creates a sense of separation, man from God, and giving him an independent power, a rebellious nature...rebelling against his own nature. This leads to the further malignant belief that man got himself into a mess and must therefore extricate himself. Which leads to failure, defeat and despair. This is called guilt or condemnation. The presence of this is the "strength of disease and sin"[135] leading to self- destruction.

If you don't know math, and you attempt to work out a problem, you will put in the place of orderly numbers and conclusions a chaotic, confused arrangement of numbers. A disaster in conclusion will ensue.

Our bodies, created by perfection, are perfect. Unable to fall into disrepair.

Our bodies are a visible product of Divine Order, harmony and intelligence. Unable to be otherwise.

But we have put this very malignant thought into

that space we call consciousness...we believe we are personally responsible to maintain and sustain our bodies in perfect order because we don't believe they are created that way and are maintained by the Spirit of Eternal Life.

God is not reactive:

Although many have both stated and written that God reacts to the evil that men do by punishing them, this is clearly a misperception of the ways and nature of God. We must not, absolutely must not, judge anything about God by looking at anything that has appeared on the visible scene. So far we have interpreted God by what appears to the human perception. But that has for centuries led men to believe in a wrathful, punishing God, man reaching no other plausible explanation for the evils that befall mankind. We have then changed the truth of God into a lie and taught ourselves and our children to be afraid of God...who is only pure goodness. This has led to lifetimes of alienation from the care and provision that God always brings to every human need. Why? Because believing these lies has caused us to not easily receive from our kind and loving Creator...not knowing that "according to our belief we have drawn our own experiences."[136] And, "as a man thinks in his heart, so is he."[137]

We cannot pray with any conviction and certainty to a God that we believe caused the problem in the first place. We live in fear of doing anything that might make God react to us and cause us harm. We miss the joy and delight that the freedom from fear brings throughout our lives. Worst of all we never know if what we pray for will ever appear. God is interpreted as fickle and not someone we can fully trust. Is it any wonder that we are told to "acquaint thyself with him and be at peace, so shall thy good come unto thee?"[138]

Our entire experience will be elevated beyond our imaginations and expectations when we learn, deep in our hearts of love that God is only good and can appear in and through his creation as pure goodness.

CHAPTER EIGHT

INTENTION

We are hearing so much these days about the "power of intention." The way it is being explained is that it is the power of God to bring forth whatever we choose...in essence, because we "are" the Divine Nature. We can simply "intend" or state whatever we want and it will appear.

Other than the fact that it makes God out to be our personal Santa Claus, I have two problems with that. One is that it doesn't work, and if it happens to, we suffer the consequences of whatever we demanded to appear. Psalms 106:15 says, that in cases like this, "He (God) will grant our demand...but along with it will come leanness to our souls." We might get it but it will be our destruction. Have you ever really demanded...or most likely begged...for something to appear in your life and when it did it turned out to be a heap of ashes?

This doctrine causes man to become self indulgent and self absorbed. As if this attitude in the heart of man isn't already overwhelming enough! We presume to know what will bless us and how it should appear, not taking into account that the Wisdom of God is so far above the presumed wisdom of man that we are "playing with fire."

This, of course, has nothing to do with man receiving what is desired and even needed from God. It is a different attitude.

On one hand we remember that we are created beings totally dependent upon the ever present and vast goodness of our Creator. In love and gratitude we "make our requests known unto God,"[139] and He in turn blesses us beyond what we could ever do ourselves...if we leave the details up to him.

But on the other hand, the attitude of man waving his wand of intention and insisting that he gets what he has demanded...is man his own God? Does man presume to know the vast Eternal Wisdom of God? Does man even know the intention and individual purpose of God in his being created and sent here in the first place? Does he care? Who's in charge here? Is this really "the new thought understanding" or the greatest expression of the pride and arrogance of man we have ever heard?

The second problem I have with this as it is being taught, is that we are not God. We are not "the Divine Nature in expression", just needing for us to awaken to it and learn how to "be god." Just because we have the capacity to be an expression of the attributes, character and power of this Eternal Life we call God, doesn't make us God! It's heard all over now and it is beyond ignorant and way beyond outrageous!

Here is the pure truth about man's relationship to God and how it is to be expressed.

"Man is but a vapor, here today and gone tomorrow."[140] Even science declares that we are some 90% water! A vapor!

But God has chosen to reveal himself through what he has made. What is formed, what is seen, is not eternal, it is temporal. It is not God. But what is formed reveals what formed it. All of the characteristics, nature, purpose and power of God is revealed by what he has made. Psalm 19:1-2 boldly proclaims, "The heavens declare the Glory of God and the firmament shows his handiwork. Day unto day utters speech and night unto night shows his knowledge." And again in Romans 1:8 we read, "For the invisible things of God are clearly seen, being understood by that which has been made." This tells us that we can know God, see him in the depths of our knowing, by seeing what is made. God reveals himself through, not as, his creation. We must learn to see him then in everything formed by him.

I had a friend once who was a sketch artist. A really good one. She would sit and doodle with a pencil and pad of paper and turn out the most detailed and perfect work I had ever seen. Once after she drew a bird on a branch I asked her why she could do that and I, on the other hand, could not? She gave a quick and decisive reply, "Because you have never seen a bird!" I protested, "Yes, of course, I have seen a bird." But she simply repeated the same words, "You have never really seen a bird or you could do this also."

We look at things, at people. But do we really see them. We must learn to see with our hearts. We must see by feeling. It is only then that we will be able to "feel" something about God being revealed.

God is Life. The Spirit of the Life of every living thing. This Spirit flows to, into, through and back to its origin. "For of him and to him and through him are all things."[141] Again, Genesis, Chapter 1 speaks of the "firmament being divided in two...and dry land appearing in the midst." Thus the dry land is creation, all that is visibly seen...and the heavens, containing the fullness of God, is both within and without, above and below. It is the Life and true substance of everything formed. But the thing formed exists as an avenue, that the true Life may be expressed. As this Life is allowed to flow to and through us, it both defines and manifests its Presence and power. That doesn't make the thing formed divine...even though Divinity is able to consume it, reveal it, define it and manifest itself as it.

As a matter of fact, the less you see of the visible the more you will see of the Divine!

The teaching that came through Jesus was both to describe the Spirit of Life and to show us how it is to be revealed. Jesus said that we should be willing to "lose the human life in exchange for the Divine Life.[142] However if we cling to the idea of personal self expression we are clinging to "our life"...and we will lose it altogether." He said even he, of himself, was incapable of doing the works that were seen through him. He taught that the wind blew where it would and we must follow the direction of that wind if we would know Eternal Life.[143]

He said "Why do you call me good (God)? Only one is good and that is God."[144] He certainly never referred to himself as the Origin and Source of all. Instead he lived a life completely free of "self" so that the fullness of the Life Divine could have the greatest and freest expression.

"I must decrease so that he can increase."[145] This in no way infers that man is God. On the contrary, God is expressed through man as man is willing to shut up and sit down! Stop wanting to be seen of men.[146] Stop insisting on being something and begin to realize the nothingness of man as a vapor, not able to change a single hair on his head.[147] As this is humbly done the greatest thing ever seen appears...God revealing himself through that man! Cease declaring yourselves! Let God declare you as he declared Jesus, "This is my beloved Son."[148]

So we gain by the willingness to lose. We go up by being willing to go down. We express the power and Presence of God as we become the seed that falls to the ground and is willing to "die" to its own imagined glory.

So now what becomes of the idea of intention? God, himself, intends. As he purposes and intends, it always comes to pass. That purpose and intention appears in our hearts and minds as a desire. Instead of insisting on the desire, let us realize that it is there because God, himself, has intended for it to appear! Let us humbly and trustingly know that our desires are God's intentions and he will bring it to pass! "Delight yourself in him, trust also in him and he shall bring it to pass."[149] "You have given him his heart's desire and not withheld the request of his lips."[150]

It takes far less assertiveness and far more yielding to see and feel and express the power of God to bring Life forth as a desire fulfilled, as a healing taking place, as anything appearing in the beauty of Divine Order which was once seen as confusion, destruction and chaos..

What have you held secretly, deep in your heart perhaps for years? Have you lost all hope of it ever happening? Is there a disease or condition that you have never been able to heal? Is there a character trait that is so undesirable to you that you attempt to hide it from sight? Has it brought the unwanted guest of condemnation to your door again and again?

Doesn't it feel ridiculous to declare yourself as God when all this remains?

Instead of giving up, instead of intending, affirming, insisting...why not simply LET. Let the winds of the Spirit of Life flow. Let it flow out to thinking well of others. Let it flow out to speaking well of others. Let it flow out to speaking peace and hope to others. Let it envelop others in the cherishing love of Spirit unto their good. Let it pour, let it flow, let it be. The longer it is allowed to freely express itself, to freely blow through you, the more content you become in whatsoever state you find yourself. It almost feels as though you don't really care about what was so very important to you once. And just about the time you are lost in the Presence of Eternal Love and Life...just about the time you are bursting with this love and life as it flows through you...the eternally intended desire appears! The pure intention of Eternal Life, desiring to express its goodness, richness and fullness, appears as the very desire of your heart revealed.

In this there is no human striving, no doubts, no terror. When the human is subdued, the Life can do nothing except appear. Remember the tiny sprout of new life that silently remains deep within the crusted shell. It is content because it knows that through its trusting, it will soon appear, manifesting a whole new resurrected Life.

There is no doubt that goodness will appear. Remember that "the rain falls on the just and unjust alike and the sun shines on the good and evil as well."[151] You are never being blessed for good behavior or punished for bad behavior. What is the factor that always causes good to appear then? The ever present Eternal Life. If the human is silenced the fullness of LIFE and all that it contains must be realized. It is always flowing, always available. Like the wind, it blows on everyone and everything alike. We are either in the position of receiving it, blowing to and through us, or we are busy trying to make something happen. Which is frank unbelief. When that is happening, the human effort to "achieve" to "do it right" is a barrier to the simple flow.

So then God, Eternal Life, is not doing anything, but simply being all that it is.

The word Sabbath actually means the "rest of God." God rested or ceased from any effort on the Sabbath. He finished his work and let flow what he had put in place. Now the fullness of him, Eternal Life, is everywhere, blessing every life, every person, every aspect of creation that allows it to flow. To "keep the Sabbath holy"[152] then is to pull back deep within you and silence all activity of doing or activity of thought, reasoning, and intellectualizing. And realize that by ceasing from your own works, (Hebrews, Chapter.4, verse 9) you can feel the overwhelming Presence of the Glory of Life everywhere. By silently acknowledging this, humbly bowing before it in your mind and heart, you release it to appear. When it does, it heals, corrects, orders, and empowers.

Every word Jesus taught was the Spirit of Life declaring to us the true nature of Itself. Every healing he did was the Spirit of Life demonstrating the nature and power of Eternal Life Itself. The Eternal Spirit was able to use his voice, his heart and mind, his existence because he chose for that to happen. He answered the call, "Here I am, send me!"[153] He became the Lamb of God. What is the nature of the Lamb? Subservient, humble, trusting, never seeking his own, never forcing his own way, and lovingly following the Voice that speaks to him all along the way. Knowing that is the Voice that loves me, cherishes me above everything else, feeds me, clothes me, teaches me, directs and guide me in Its Wisdom, and takes care of my young. It fulfills my every desire, for its intention is my desire!

"My sheep hear my voice and no other voice will they follow."[154] "And they followed the Lamb whithersoever he led them."[155] Now we, by choice, become the lamb.

So God, Eternal Life, is not doing. It is simply being. God is not healing, not fixing, not directing, but just BEING all that it is and when that blows freely through your humble and waiting heart, everything suddenly appears in overwhelming goodness.

Spirit of Prophecy:

Have you ever wondered how God could say that if you "delighted yourself in him," he would give you "the desires of your heart?"[156] Or in Psalm 21, how he promises that all of our requests would be fulfilled?

What assurance do we really have that our requests will be granted? How can he say this to us before he even knows what our requests will be? Why is it that some always receive their requests and others fail to do so? Is God biased towards some? Of course not! Did some earn it and others not? By grace we receive, never by human works! How do we deal with doubts and unbelief?

There are principles here that must be known.

The first is opening ourselves to Eternal Wisdom that is ours for the asking. When we trust that his Life is actually our Eternal Life and we know then that only goodness can appear, we must ask for Wisdom in our choice of desires. What is God's best here? What will fulfill his eternal intention? What is in the Divine Mind? If we ask for Wisdom, Wisdom will certainly come. Otherwise we find ourselves groping in the dark and fearful, needing to know the future in order to make the right decisions. The lack of confidence will cause us to be defeated. But confidence comes with hearing and responding to Divine Wisdom. "Faith cometh by hearing and hearing by the word of God."[157]

We must ask for Wisdom in making our requests. We will then ask according to his perfect knowledge and purpose. We must ask to know his mind in any given situation. Just to name a few of the examples in my own life, "Are my daughters ok? Will this endeavor I am embarking upon be fruitful? Is this person's life threatened with this affliction? Is this the right direction?" Many threats and challenges have come but I always ask, "Should I be concerned here? Is there anything you want me to do here? Is there something I need to know here? Will this be a problem?"

Has it occurred to us that since we are truly one with him, (read John, chapter 17) his mind is actually our mind, his heart actually our heart? Consequently we have direct access to his mind. One way he communicates to us his purpose and intention is by causing us to feel a desire towards something. In reality it is really his heart that we are feeling as our own. The understanding and acceptance of this will forever cause us to soar with certainty in every situation we encounter.

Instead of wringing our hands in dread that we might not receive what we desire or need, we must ask him, "Is this what you want? Am I feeling this because you have placed this in my heart?" This is a sure way not to go off on our own tangent unto destruction or defeat. This is how we will know for certain that what we have desired will be granted to us. And once we know this, we enter into what the Bible refers to as the Spirit of prophecy, certain of what is to come. Our desires are a reflection of his intentions.

By definition prophecy is foretelling a future event. God warns us in Ezekiel, chapter 13, never to presumptuously declare or prophesy using him as an authority unless you have specifically heard, and are confident you have heard, from God. This is why we must ask, ask, ask. "How should I pray about this? How will this turn out? What should I say? What attitude of the heart is your heart in this situation? Which way should I go?" Then when the answer is clear, the confidence we carry is the power to release the fulfillment of the desire! All doubts fade into nothingness. No one can inject us with their dread or fear. Instead we become the influencing factor for good in the hearts of others.

There are those who teach the "name it, claim it" doctrine. If we but "say it, it is ours." Then when what they claimed fails to materialize, they sink into confusion and despair. We must always remember that even though we are eternally ONE with the Divine, we are sent here to serve a purpose greater than our own. We are not here to satisfy every self indulgent idea. We are here to serve the Most High God in his purpose to reveal heaven here and now, on earth, in us and through his entire creation. Humility must never be forsaken as we strive to move into our role as kings in his kingdom. The authority needed to dissolve the works of darkness comes by hearing the Voice of Spirit and obeying it.

So, as in everything having to do with the things of God, there is a balance. "God is a God of just weights and balances."[158] There is no way to get around seeking God and his purpose and will for anything and everything.

Remember the words of the greatest spiritual authority ever to appear on the human scene...the One sent to teach us how to do it ourselves. "I can of my own self do nothing. As I hear, that I do."[159]

The Centurion soldier who came to Jesus to heal his servant (Luke, Chapter 7) spoke such deep words of understanding of this principle when he said, "I, too, am a man under authority, and there are those under my command...therefore I know if you but speak the word my servant will be healed."[160]

No amount of power and authority will ever be withheld from us as we stay in the Divine Order God has established. He is our authority. We, then, have the depth of certainty to be the sure authority over all evil.

Another principle is to release some of the weighty ideas and thoughts which have acted as a block to receiving our desires and needs. This is not to analyze what we are thinking. It is not to search out the origin of our beliefs and fears. It is not to find a cause for them either. The simplicity of just choosing to let all barriers and blockages fall to the ground at your feet...like shedding a heavy garment might feel... and then standing in stillness for a moment to realize the emerging of the clean, free Presence of Spirit as it is released from your soul. An "open door" to receiving!

This leads to the next principle, which is to open ourselves to receiving the goodness of Eternal Life, by way of thanksgiving. You will find that this is the sure way of receiving what is needed and that in abundance. This is discussed in the chapter entitled "Releasing the Flow of the Spirit of God."

CHAPTER NINE

RELEASING THE FLOW
OF THE SPIRIT OF GOD

So now by the grace of God we understand that we are here as manifestations of all that God is. God is Eternal Life…never having a beginning nor an ending. Contained within this vastness are all the attributes that we attribute to God. We come from that. The idea in the Divine Mind is that the fullness of this be revealed out from the very midst of us.

We have also learned the first and greatest lesson of all and that is that we don't do this. We can't do this. We were never expected to do this. The abject failure of the early Israelites to obtain their goal (promised land) taught us this with no uncertainty. Jesus said that he also could not do this ("I can of my own self do nothing").[161] The humility of this heart-attitude is what releases the Spirit of God, the Spirit of Eternal Life through us and enables us to become the full manifestation of all that God is. By ceasing from our own efforts we make a space for grace to appear. The realm of grace exists far above the realm of human effort constrained under the law of cause and effect.

Once we are experiencing the law of grace, all consequences we may have accrued vanish!

So how does this happen? What is our responsibility...or better put, our response to all this? How do we cooperate without giving in to the temptation of thinking we must do something?

As long as we trust our abilities more than we trust the goodness of God and his ever present intention to do us only good, we will struggle to cease from our efforts. But once we are acquainted with his true nature and once we fully embrace the realization that only goodness and perfection can be experienced from God, we will gladly say with Jesus, "I can of my own self do nothing,"[162] and watch as the flow of the Spirit of Eternal Life fills that space we provided and "makes all things new."[163]

We are given a key to consistent success both spiritually and in our human affairs. It is found all through the Bible stories and admonitions. It is choosing a heart full of gratitude instead of a perpetual heart of "needs," "wants," "don't haves" and "please give me." We live our lives forever looking at what we don't have. We memorize every scripture that promises God will "give us what we want or ask." We have not yet realized how that closes down the perpetual flow of abundance. Yes, we will "get" but at the cost of needing to "get something else" tomorrow. Choosing to live from the kingdom of God instead of the kingdom of loss, lack, fear and insecurity, we remember that we contain the wholeness of all goodness deep within us. We came with this. This is the substance of all that exists, all that we are. So if we know this we will choose to live out from gratitude and joy, thus allowing the doors of our heart to be fully open, allowing the goodness to flow and the human condition to reflect that goodness and order.

Let's look at some of the examples we have found in our Bible.

Paul and Silas were in a dark, damp prison awaiting execution in the morning.[164] They could have prayed and wailed and begged for deliverance and probably would have received it. But they knew that in the flow of the Spirit of Life…through them…they would prove their trust in the Wisdom of God. So they sang and worshipped and praised the Wisdom of God and thereby released the Spirit. They were "sold out." They belonged to the flow of God. God was worthy to be praised no matter what. It is said that the jail house shook and the prison doors opened as a result of the earth quaking from the roaring of the Spirit's response to their devotion and trust. All the prisoners escaped and the jailor was converted as well. This of course speaks of the opening of the prison of our souls that true freedom of the Eternal Life might be revealed.

Jonah found himself deep in the "belly of hell"[165] as a result of the self condemnation he felt for not heeding the voice of direction from Divine Mind. The Voice spoke to declare its intention and purpose. Jonah yielded instead to a haughty self righteousness and refused to heed. Soon the dark blanket of despair covered his soul. There was no escaping it. But in the darkness of the hour Jonah "remembered the Lord." He thought of the goodness, the forgiveness, the mercy and the faithfulness even when he was not so faithful. He chose to stop looking at the mess he made and instead look at the immutable nature of the compassionate, eternal God. "Those who observe lying vanities (evil appearances) forsake their own mercies." (Jonah 2:8) He would look away from what was wrapping itself around his soul to suffocate out the very life (if it even could). He would look at the faithfulness of God. He would look so long and so hard that the delight of it would fill his soul instead of the dread of evil. He "offered the sacrifice of thanksgiving." It is referred to as a sacrifice because it is very difficult to look away from the threats of evil and the horror it declares and find the God who is always there. When he did, God, the Spirit of Love which no evil can stand against, caused Jonah to find the place of safety and quietness he so desperately needed. And so he was free.

The three Hebrew men spoken of in the Book of Daniel[166] were to be thrown into the "fiery furnace," turned up seven times hotter than usual because they refused to acknowledge and follow after the "god of this world." They were given one last chance to change their minds. Instead of focusing on the agony that awaited them, they turned their focus to the Nature of the God they served. They knew and declared his faithfulness, his purpose that reigned supreme, his power over all the works of darkness. They were prepared to die if necessary. If so, they would die acknowledging the uninterrupted goodness of God. They walked into and through the fire but they were lifted into the dimension of the Only Begotten Son of God. Consequently they felt nothing of the fire that surrounded them. They were not harmed. They were free from any devises of evil. Their choice to elevate the nature of God rather than elevate the works of darkness proved to be all it took to place them in the safety and security they needed!

And so is the power of those who, instead of first accepting the evil as real and powerful...then asking God to fix what has been acknowledged as real...they learn instead to release the mighty flow of the Eternal Spirit of Life and let it proclaim its unmatched power.

There are those who say that when one is full of gratitude that acts as a boomerang and comes back to them as goodness. Others describe it as a magnet, attracting good. But looking at the theme of releasing the magnificent Life from within, I would say that being filled with delight of the beauty and richness of the Divine Life actually opens up the heart and out flows the creative aspect of Spirit, bringing to manifestation all that is needed for the fullness of God to appear.

Consider Jesus at the multiplying of the loaves and fishes.[167] First he had everyone sit down. Sitting down is declaring that I am not striving anymore about anything. I am at rest. I am in a very calm and peaceful state knowing that all is well. No matter the appearance of lack of whatever, I do not live by appearances. Following this he looked up to Heaven. In doing so he was acknowledging all abundance and goodness comes from the eternal Source. Then he "gave thanks." By this he was declaring his certainty that all that is ever needed is continually flowing and filling all space. The peaceful realization and joy that he felt opened his heart to release the creative substance of the eternal Spirit...thus satisfying the need.

"By prayer and supplication, **with thanksgiving**, let your requests be made known to your father (Source)."[168]

"In everything give thanks."[169]

"Being thankful for this very thing, that he which began this good work in you will perform it until the day that Jesus Christ is revealed."[170]

"Delight yourself in the Lord and He will give you the desires of your heart."[171]

Thanksgiving is being filled with the awareness of perpetual goodness. You cannot be overjoyed at the goodness of God and be wringing your hands at the same time. You must look away from the picture that threatens your good. You must look towards that which is constant and can never change.

Thanksgiving is the key to an open heart, by which we release the fullness of all that God is, which brings great joy, contentment and abundance. There is no image of horror that will not be corrected.

I remember several years ago a baby was snatched from the mother in a parking lot while she was trying to get her other children into the car. She ran after the car, holding onto the bumper, being dragged along until she had to let go. She and her husband belonged to a Pentecostal Church that builds its structure on the power of the Spirit to save. They knew they must praise and worship to allow the Spirit to flow out from them. They knew that by doing so they were declaring that God is faithful. They would look to that and choose to trust. Their whole church gathered together and sang and worshipped all night. Even with tears they continued. The next day the woman who took the baby showed up at her mother's house announcing that the baby was hers. The mother called the police and the baby was safely home in twenty-four hours.

Remember when King David finally took the throne and decided that the first thing he must do was to recover the Ark of the Covenant from their enemies.[172] The Ark symbolized the presence of God to them and assured them of safety and blessings forever. But when he attempted to bring it back things didn't go well. He knew he was missing something. He returned to Jerusalem to pray and ask for counsel. This was what he heard. He was to appoint singers, musicians, dancers, those who would praise and worship to go before the whole company of Israelites as well as the Ark. They thus led the Ark all the way back to Jerusalem with great joy and with great protection all the way.

Jehoshaphat, king of Judah, was to go out to battle.[173] The enemies that stood before them were a thousand times greater in number than they, but he learned from David's situation years before. He placed the singers, the musicians, the trumpeters to go before them, praising the Lord as they went. The enemies turned on each other and finally fled. They won without a battle.

This is a principle that can no longer be ignored. I encourage you to pray specifically about this, asking for clear direction and especially that the door of your heart to be open and free. By this you will surely see the abundant goodness of the God you have come to love and to serve.

"I will enter his gates with thanksgiving in my

heart. I will enter his courts with praise."[174] Once you find yourself deep in the place of the very Presence of God, your heart will be filled to overflowing with a Spirit of Gratitude and you will know contentment for the very first time in your life. This is the open door to receiving it all!

CHAPTER TEN

JUST WHAT IS THIS LIFE ALL ABOUT?

So let's summarize what we have learned here. Why are we here? What is the end result and what is our response (notice I did not say responsibility) in all this?

One thing is for sure, we are not here to get, to achieve, to be humanly fulfilled. All this will come as we stop focusing on it and begin to set our total affection on the real reason we are here. It is true that God will give us the desires of our heart, but it will not bring us satisfaction like we thought it would. We will always want something else, something more. This is because we are not yet joining with the Spirit to find our true desire.

We know now that we are a manifestation of Eternal Life. Again a Life that had no beginning and will have no end. Incidentally, the word beginning found in the first chapter of Genesis, "In the beginning, God..." actually refers to "the head, the source, the chief, the highest."

We know now that we were sent by the will of the Wisdom and intention of the Source of Eternal Life. That Source has a purpose and it is intact, no matter what else appears. God will have his way.

We have heard the interpretations of man via various religious voices throughout the centuries and this has caused us and the whole of mankind confusion beyond description. But I want us to turn our attention to one eternal, dynamic Divine purpose and focus on that.

We are to here to manifest the fullness of God. And this will happen. This is called being the Christ of God. Jesus was the forerunner and example of not only how this would appear but how to realize this. This will be achieved by one way only. A new identity. A new concept of ourselves. Not as "another truth" but as an entire shift in perception and soul, away from the human to the Divine.

When that happens all the confusion, the chaos, the disease, the sadness and grief...all human pain will be dissolved and we will be standing in paradise. We will be the radiant glory of God. Paul writes a lot about it in 1 Corinthians. He talks about the "first Adam," the human, mortal nature, being swallowed up by the appearing of the "last Adam," which is the Christ nature.[175] This is the second coming we hear so much about. The emerging of something eternal and holy, appearing out from the depths of our souls, dissolving entirely the confused and darkened humanity. "This mortal must "put on" (an unfortunate choice of words here) immortality and this corruptible must "put on" (again unfortunate imagery) incorruption."[176] The idea of "putting on" leads us to believe that we must reach out and get hold of something we don't have. It also gives us the strong idea that we are responsible to do something here. Hence the birthing of so many conflicting doctrines and concepts.

Once we feel responsible, we begin to feel failure. We really don't know what is required...even after we have "done it all" we yet feel that there is always more we haven't done. With failure comes condemnation and the expectation of punishment...hence "hell" and suffering... hence disease, loss, lack and general human misery. It is well to remember that the Israelites spent thousands of years trying to "please God and do it right" and yet have never gained much more than conflict, wars, hatred and defeat.

The very atmosphere is full of "self help" programs. Even religions have attempted to use these as ways to achieve holiness...or at least make the human appear better. Although being better is preferable to being worse, still this is not the way to the new identity. This is like rearranging furniture in a house that has already been condemned. John the Baptist presented a consciousness of "bringing forth fruits worthy to be accepted."[177] More human effort! But Jesus announced a new birthing altogether. Later Jesus would declare that "there was never one so great born of a woman than John, but still he was least in the kingdom of God."[178] Why did he say that? Because he was still one born of a woman...a human identity trying to be a better human. Only a new identity can be found in this kingdom of God or Paradise of God. All the goodness we can humanly achieve will yet cause us to be found on the outside looking in.

Every religion has its "ways and means" to bring

forth this desired Life. Keeping the "Sacraments" is one. Answering the "altar call" is another. Being baptized "in the Spirit" is another. Living in seclusion from the "world," fasting, endless affirmations and reaffirmations.

Jesus gave us the clearest, most constructive instructions as to how paradise, here on earth, is to be achieved. And as you would imagine, it starts with the individual who seeks it first. We seek it because the Spirit of this Eternal Life begins to stir deep in our souls and will not let up until it is completed. "For you have not chosen me but I have chosen you, called you and ordained that you would bring forth (fruit) the manifestation of this Life."[179] "Behold, I have called you by name, you are mine."[180] Before you came forth from the womb you were designed to be one in whom this great event would be completed. This was by the will of him who formed you and sent you. To whom you belong throughout eternity. You did not choose this. Again, "Behold, I have chosen you. You have not chosen me."[181]

To help us get the picture of how this coming forth into our true nature is to happen we look at that which we see every day. For instance, the sun arises out from the midst of the blackened sky...everyday. Out of death appears life. The springtime of new life bursts forth out from the cold, bleak winter...every year. Out of death appears life. Babies appear out from the dark recesses of the human womb...daily, hourly. Out of death appears life. New life appears, fresh and vibrant and always out from an appearance of desolation or death (human, mortality). Jesus, the Savior of the whole world, appeared first in a smelly, dirty manger, in a cold, dark, wintery night. Out from death appears life. Later, once his body was certainly dead, he appeared in a new life form. All this tells us something certain. What we look for will appear…right out from the midst of our uncertainty, our failures, our defeats and sufferings…and we are no more responsible for this to happen than we are for the sun to shine or the spring to come.

The most wonderful analogy given to us is that of a seed. Jesus said that unless a seed falls into the ground and dies, "it abides alone."[182] But if it dies it will bring forth one hundred fold, in this life, right here on earth. No seed has ever sprouted until it is placed deep in the earth, quiet and silently waiting till the Life within it has filled the space provided and it bursts forth. It can no longer be contained. Life will not be denied. But because we have misunderstood what he meant by "dying" we assumed he was declaring the need for suffering. Nothing could be further from the truth.

In order to receive anything new we must "die" to what has been held prior in thought. In order to climb another rung on Jacob's ladder we must leave the last rung behind. In order to ever see the appearing of harmony and perfection in any of our affairs we must let go of our will and our way and allow the Spirit full access to achieve what we have desired. If that produces suffering it is because we are not trusting the Spirit to do for us what we cannot…and therefore we are clinging to what has not worked. Once we say in our hearts, "I trust you. I know you will fulfill this desire, heal this confusion, and cause your strength to appear where sickness and pain has dominated. I know your intention is to appear through me, as me, to reveal perfection and beauty and a life of joy. No matter what, I choose to trust you." At that point all tension, anguish, depression, despair, worry, fretting and doubt will disappear. A certainty will begin to creep into your soul. The "suffering" is over. You will not know the way he takes, but you will be confident that he is forging a way to appear, right in the space that before was occupied by frantic human efforts of some sort.

The same Spirit of Eternal Life that holds the earth on its axis, causes the tide to come in and go out, brings the earth its sunshine daily, makes the seed to bring forth harvest, is the same Spirit that fills the substance of your being and has forever. It is responsible, capable, and fully committed to continuing to bring forth Life.

The "you" that you have been identifying with is but a very thin covering. Just beneath the surface is the fullness of God. The Eternal Holiness. The Spirit of Eternal Life. Who and what you are and have always been. It is your substance. Not flesh and bones. Not all the trappings of this mortal life...but the Spirit of Life. The same Life that holds the worlds in their place. The same Life of every living animal and creature, plant and tree and blade of grass. The intelligence of all the earth and universe. Once we learn the absoluteness of this, it is left then to learn how to "go with the flow of it." We must find that place where our desires and the intentions of Spirit are one and the same. We must learn as the Centurion soldier told Jesus...that we are under this authority (Spirit) and as we yield to this we become an authority over our entire environment (including our bodies) and every aspect of creation.[183] A very profound understanding. And a very accessible place for us to live from.

To access this is as simple as turning your focus onto it...instead of continually onto the confusion of the human existence. We bring forth what we give our attention to. This has been a principle of life forever. No matter what crazy thing you are dealing with or worrying about, just say, "Not my will. Not my way. No matter what, I trust you. You already occupy this space with your fullness. Do what is perfect. I will not look away from you. I will trust. And you will appear."

It is hard to look away from whatever is dancing in front of you trying to hold your attention...only to destroy you for looking. But Wisdom lifts up her voice and cries out to you, "Look unto me and be ye saved."[184] Jeremiah declares many times that, "You cannot enter the gates of Jerusalem (holy place) carrying any burden." You cannot even rehearse it to God in prayer. Only look to his vastness, his greatness, his gentleness and his faithfulness...and enter in. When you emerge later you will find "all things new."[186]

No matter what aspect of your life is being challenged, look directly at that space until you actually FEEL that the fullness of God is already there, in beauty, order and perfection. It needs no help from you or anyone else. It will come forth. It will appear. It will "make all things new."[187]

This idea of trust is actually the fulfillment of the command to "keep holy the Sabbath."[188] Man worked for six days...the seventh day is the day we cease from all our futile efforts and ego building antics and let God appear. Only when we quit thinking...endless thinking about our problems, can Spirit have access. We are strongly admonished by Isaiah, in chapter 30, to cease from our own efforts, to cease from looking to "man" for our help and to sit still. "In quietness and confidence shall be your strength. Sit still."[189] The stillness of meditation, deeply remembering that the very substance of us is only Spirit and that Spirit already occupies whatever space seems to be in conflict right now, will immediately do more for us than all the endless running around in circles, frantic and afraid. This is how healings are achieved.

The only thing which has the power to block the Spirit appearing with the answer is you in the way. Endless thinking, endless affirmations and reciting. Endless talking. Fretting, worrying, maintaining constant vigil over the appearance of evil. Have I prayed "right?" Are my thoughts "ok?" Isn't this just us, once again, thinking we must qualify for what we need? Does it depend on us? Or does the entire scenario depend upon the undeniable nature of the faithful, merciful, compassionate, forever near and available Shepherd? If we look to him, never taking our eyes off to look at how we are doing, and keep looking at him only...we are drawing everything we need from the only Source who can fill our hearts and fix our lives. The one who promised to lead us to "green pastures," to "restore our souls,"[190] to "go before us to make the crooked ways straight,"[191] "to open every door that no man can close,"[192] "to never leave us or forsake us,"[193] to pour his entire life out to us, through us and for us. "For of him and through him and to him are all things."

In deep meditation we are receiving all this and more. We are receiving all that is necessary for the solution of the problem and that in abundance. Learn to trust. Choose to trust. Ask Spirit to enable you to trust. This is grace in action.

The Spirit flows as the wind blows. Just as we cannot know "from whence it comes or where it goes,"[194] we cannot second guess the Spirit. We must go with the flow. We must stop struggling. Stop manipulating to get what we want. Stop "outlining," telling the Spirit how it must be done. Stop rehearsing the confusion before us. Stop trying to "be acceptable" to get what we want. Stop endless wanting, wanting, wanting. The Spirit knows what you want before you do. Stop thinking about it all. Stop analyzing the present situation or past experiences. Stop the restlessness, the empty scurrying about to go nowhere.

The opposite of Life is not death, but stagnation. We intuitively must know this because we are afraid of stagnation. Hence the mortal is restless at his very core. But keeping busy is not the antidote for this. Actively entering into the flow of Spirit by deep contemplation and meditation, by letting it go ahead of us, will accomplish more in one day than all the busyness of a man's lifetime.

Quietness of the soul is the greatest posture to understanding and to receiving. Silence of the soul is the key to the power of God. Just breathe and be…and let the wind blow to you and through you. Let it reveal the greatness of God right in front of you. Feel it. Eternal Life cannot be taught as much as felt. The tide comes and the tide goes. The waters flow and the current carries whatever is in it towards a desired end. The wind blows and circles about back to its source. Ecclesiastes says that the rain falls, the rivers flow and all the water returns back to its source.[195] Learn to glide along with the purposes of God and all your needs will be met and all your desires fulfilled.

When Solomon built the temple he surrounded it with a porch.[196] This was the structure that needed to be crossed in order to enter the inner court or "throne room" of Presence and authority. Spiritually this is a place of judgment...or decision...or better put, the place of Wisdom. This is achieved by a PAUSE. When an event is pressing for a reaction...and what human event is not...this is the place where you are not reacting as a mere human, but the Holy Son of God. This is where the Holy Spirit of Wisdom speaks to the silent soul, the soul that refuses to react, and when you respond to that, you will be as the Christ of God. If you are faithful to pause, he will always be faithful to fill that space with his wisdom and his power. Then you are free to enter in to his authority (throne).

Do you see that your "Christhood" is even now available to you to be and to use whenever you choose?

Revelation tells us that we will receive a "new name."[197] This is a new nature. A new identity, different in thinking, acting and being. It tells us that no one but he who receives it shall know of it. It comes as such a sacred experience that you will not be able to talk of it. Those who "lift their voices in the streets"[198] have never entered in.

Further, it will follow after we receive a "white stone"..."and the new name will emerge from within that stone."[199] Long ago the religious leaders were also the judges, the ones who determined the guilt or innocence of a person accused. They heard the case and each man secretly placed either a white stone or a black stone in the basket passed around. The white stone was a declaration of innocence. As we leave behind (by the grace of God) the whole great deception of "original sin," every thought and idea of any human failure, sin or defeat in the past...including the whole identity of one who could live in that...we are ready to take on the new. "You must remember not the former things, neither consider the things of old. Behold (observe) I do a new thing. Shall it not spring forth? I will make a way in the wilderness (aimless wandering of the human) and rivers in the desert (place of no apparent life)."[200]

Later Jesus is very clear when he says, "The new name that you receive is MY NEW NAME."[201] Not even the identity of Jesus the man, but the Eternal Life that he represents now and forever.

God is Omnipotent. Therefore there is no opposing force. Life only will appear. God is Omnipresent. Therefore there is not two of you...only ONE.

Learn to train yourself to feeling your way through this life, instead of seeing your way. By that I mean we can see an animal, a tree, a bird, a person...or we can feel that Life within. We sense it with a heart of acceptance, compassion, tenderness and understanding. Thus we maintain our position in the Presence of God always. We begin to realize that we are seeing and experiencing Paradise right now. Heaven is sensed all around us and the whole world is safe. Even only one person doing this will bring enormous change to human conditions and situations. You will be living out from the mind and heart of God and, by this, you will begin to sense your true identity emerging. You will be filled with gratitude and contentment. You will know that you are now superior to every human condition...the idea of victimhood will be such a distant past that it will not appear in thought again.

This is between you alone and your Creator. Hold it deep within your heart, as silently and quietly as you would hold any intimate relationship. It is sacred. It is achievable. It is the purpose and Divine Intention for you being here. It is a work of the Spirit from beginning to end. It is grace. Right here. Right now.

CHAPTER ELEVEN

WISDOM

Eternal life is one of the attributes or manifestations of the Spirit of God. Also referred to as the Spirit of Life, it is that pulsating factor that vibrates throughout the world of form, bringing with it the energy and awakened consciousness to *be*. Indeed it created the world of form as it responded to the Word, or intention of the Eternal Mind.[202]

This Eternal Source, we call God, has many differing attributes and charactistics. Instead of simply calling this God, it is so much more helpful to refer to it according to its varying nature. It causes us to understand it better and to feel closer to it, such as Love, Goodness, Faithfulness, Life, etc. The core of its Mind is Wisdom. The core of its heart is Mercy. It is the Spirit that flows and animates the entire creation. It is not a man and therefore we often hesitate to refer to it as he, although it still is often done. It is Spirit and contains all the male and female attributes combined as one.

Religion has God outside of us with rules to be

obeyed if we would "please" him. But remembering that heaven is both within and without as spoken in Genesis, chapter 1, we must learn to find this dynamic Presence deep within our being. Therefore to understand God, to actually have an intimate relationship with him, we must turn within.

There is a Wisdom coming from the heart of God that is always flowing, always available and if sought will always be found. We will need to turn our attention to the heaven within though to find it. Wisdom resides in the deepest chamber of the soul of man. It is simple to access, but unless we know it is there and easily accessed, we can go through our entire life and miss it completely. The results of missing it are the many devastations we see today all about us, such as human conflict, disease, poverty, wars, corruption, greed and the like. In the absence of Divine Wisdom man responds to his circumstances in a reactionary way, which more often than not, is not particularly helpful. While religion is satisfied to "keep the rules" and then just muddle through life doing the "best we can," believing all the horrors we encounter comes from this separate God, we have found that this Wisdom will direct our thoughts and our emotions and guide us safely through life, blessing us and covering us as we go. As we learn to let it be our guide, day by day, decision by decision, we find our way is a way of peace, delight and fulfillment. That then, is the only "rule."

There is a difference between wisdom and understanding. Understanding is a factor of the mind, the intellect, while wisdom is the substance of the heart. Understanding the spiritual principles we live by is only relevant to us if we learn by wisdom how to actually put them into practice and then allow the Spirit that flows to go before us to cause these principles to be activated.

I often think of early on when I first began my walk with God. It was when my second daughter was born and if you remember from my first book, *"Of Monkeys and Dragons,"* she suffered severe deprivation of oxygen for several days and this affected her brain function. She was consequently diagnosed as severely mentally retarded, blind in one eye, compromised pulmonary function, and multitudes of other problems. At that point I had never considered God, and wasn't even sure if he existed; If so, I concluded, he didn't care much for us as evidenced by the suffering and anguish I witnessed all around. But even before my first encounter with God I intuitively knew several things that did not line up with the medical mentality surrounding us. One was that if I never spoke of her as being afflicted, if I never let anyone around us speak of it, somehow, someway, someday she would be ok. I would think of her as normal, I would treat her as normal. And three years later she was definitely normal. From head to toe.

Now how did I know that was a strong spiritual principle? "Always look in the direction that you want to see appear." Even though I never knew Wisdom, Wisdom knew me. There is a scripture that brings tears to my eyes every time I think of it. Isaiah 65:1 says, "I am found of them that sought me not." While the whole religious world places the burden of relationship with God on us, God places it on himself. He seeks us. He chooses us. He will have us.

But when Wisdom does speak, it compels us to respond. Recently a mother of a late teenage daughter called asking for help to heal her daughter who suddenly lost the vision in one eye, completely. Having learned years ago to wait for the direction of Wisdom for every situation I remained silent while she spoke about the problem. I knew a couple of things right away. One was that they must come to the clinic and that when they did I would know what to do, as well as what caused it. But the mother's reaction to my words was disappointment. She wanted to know why the daughter couldn't just be healed spiritually. Why was it necessary to travel all that way and submit to something physical? At the time I could only say that this was the direction I was receiving. Oftentimes the answer is that there is something other than what is appearing that needs to be healed and just shooting for the quick fix is not going to do it.

There are principles of living in this kingdom of God that when we find them out and commit to live by them, (only by the ability of the Spirit...grace) we find perpetual goodness on our way. It's much like the driving laws. If we learn them and also learn to drive with an unselfish regard for others, we will be less likely to ever have an accident. But, conversely, if we never learn them or just choose to ignore them, we are certainly more likely to have an incident on the highways.

She finally committed to coming down but I knew the daughter was not really in agreement with the decision. It took less than fifteen minutes to learn what physically caused the blindness as well as what spiritual principles were being grossly violated. But there would have been no way to heal her as long as she continued holding the haughty and defiant attitude she came in with. Why? Because she was not in the state of humility that would have caused her to be receptive to the flow of the Spirit. God isn't Santa Claus. We don't just demand a healing. "A humble and a contrite heart, Oh God, you will not despise."[203] "Before destruction, the heart of a man is haughty. Before honor is humility."[204] We can never expect to be able to receive Wisdom unless we are at a place of letting go of our own ways and means and demanding outcomes.

The answers from Wisdom were clear. And if adhered to, my expectation of healing was also clear. But the young girl was having nothing to do with it all and left. In this case the healing had to begin with the healing of the soul. This is the difference between understanding and wisdom. We can know it all, or not, but when we shut down the flow of the Spirit of Life and let the sometimes defiant will of man to lead out, the results will most certainly be destruction. We want what we want. But this is clearly a stone that must be "rolled away"[205] for the fullness of Life to appear.

So what is Wisdom? It is best understood by describing what it is not.

There is the way of man which is called wisdom, but it is not eternal Wisdom. The results will be a roll of the dice, at best, and we know it. Therefore we are afraid of our own decisions, uncertain of the outcome. We unknowingly sabotage our successes. "There is a way that seems right to a man but the end thereof is death."[206]

Wisdom is not looking at your options and coming up with the best one you feel comfortable with. Wisdom is not listening to others, the internet, your family or dearest friends. Wisdom is not looking at statistics. Wisdom is not the same as intelligence. Wisdom is not the same as being educated. Wisdom is not the loudest voice or the one "in your face." Wisdom never follows the money trail. Wisdom never follows the personal desires or demands. Although if Wisdom is sought and followed, these desires will appear at the right time in the right way to secure peace and security.

Wisdom is not the same as discretion, but they are closely related. Discretion is the freedom to act in accordance with ones best judgment, usually without "reaction." Wisdom is not knowledge which appeals to the mind. However when Wisdom is employed it produces true knowledge, understanding, discretion and sound judgment. The end of following Wisdom is always success in every endeavor.

Let's read what Proverbs says about Wisdom:

"Happy is the man that finds wisdom, and the man that gets understanding. For the merchandise of it is better than the merchandise of silver, and the gain thereof than fine gold. She (Wisdom) is more precious than rubies: and all the things you can desire are not to be compared unto her. Length of days is in her right hand; and in her left hand riches and honor. Her ways are ways of pleasantness, and all her paths are peace. She is a tree of life to them that lay hold upon her: and happy is every one that retains her. The LORD by wisdom hath founded the earth; by understanding hath he established the heavens. By his knowledge the depths are broken up, and the clouds drop down the dew. My son, let not them depart from your eyes: keep sound wisdom and discretion: So shall they be life unto your soul, and grace to your neck (human will). Then shall you walk in your way safely, and your foot shall not stumble. When you lie down, you shall not be afraid: yea, you shall lie down, and your sleep shall be sweet. Be not afraid of sudden fear, neither of the desolation of the wicked, when it comes. For the LORD shall be your confidence, and shall keep your foot from being taken.[207] Get wisdom, get understanding: forget it not; neither decline from the words of my mouth. Forsake her not, and she shall preserve you: love her, and she shall keep you. Wisdom is the principal thing; therefore get wisdom: and with all your getting, get understanding. Exalt her, and she shall promote you: she shall bring you to honor, when you embrace her. She shall give to you an ornament of grace: a crown of glory shall she deliver to you. Hear, O my son, and receive my sayings; and the years of your life shall be many. I have taught you in the way of wisdom; I have led you in right paths. When you walk, your steps shall not be straitened; and when you run, you shall not stumble. Take fast hold of instruction; let her not go: keep her; for she is your life. My son, attend to my words; incline your ear unto my sayings. Let them not depart from your eyes; keep them in the midst of your heart. For they are life unto those that find them, and health to all their flesh. Keep your heart with all diligence; for out of it are the issues of life. Put away from you a haughty mouth, and perverse lips put far from you. Let your eyes look right on, and let your eyelids look straight before you. Ponder the path of your feet, and let all your ways be established. Turn not to the right hand, nor to the left: remove your foot from evil."[208]

How do we find Wisdom? How can we be sure we are hearing right? What if my will or my fear is so strong that my own heart deceives me?

These are honest questions that I have heard all my life. And in the early years, I too wrestled with myself.

1) It all has to do with the condition of your heart. Self honesty is the principle component. Do not try to hide from God whatever is lurking around your mind. Talk to him about it no matter how obtrusive it may sound to you. Once it's out there, it usually clears away.

2) To know God as a pure love that forever and ever only wants good for you is critical. If you still have even a tinge of an idea that "this suffering may be for your good, or you must have deserved it, or maybe you thought something or did something that brought this into your experience," you had better start right there. Don't try to mash it down...just talk to God about it. "I know in my head that you forgive and don't punish, but I am still afraid." "I know you are only good and can only do good to me, but all that I have been taught keeps coming up and it makes me afraid to fully trust that this is so." "I know I have not been a loving person in my life. Should I go and ask forgiveness? Have you forgiven me?" Get whatever is in the way of pure peace with God out of the way...but remem-

ber that only God can remove it. So talk to him. Be painfully honest. You pray until you have heard the Voice whisper its wisdom to your heart or until you are confident without a doubt...and that is the healing. Once it is secure in consciousness, it will surely appear in the visible world. Jesus said we must first believe that we have received something before it can appear.[209]

3) Always go to God for the truth about him...not for the healing. Every disturbance in the atmosphere of God's paradise originates with a faulty idea of the nature of God. Several years ago I was glancing through a "LIFE" magazine and saw a picture of a naked black boy, about nine years old, who could have been his birth weight. Without reading it, I knew it was depicting the devastating famine in Ethiopia. I jumped to my feet and began pacing and crying out to God. "How do I pray about this?" Several things came to my mind, but I was still so agitated that I knew it was just my mind. Then I heard. "Am I not the father of every living thing? Am I not benevolently good? Could I ever allow my children to experience such?" It stopped me. I suddenly realized that for me to accept this picture I would have to accept such horrible things about the nature of God. So I repented for what was widely accepted here. I knew the heart of God and he was right...this couldn't be it! I spent quite a bit of time with this and felt that the situation was certainly healed. And within days it was announced that the famine was over.

Another time I was with a woman who was imminently dying from breast cancer. It was quiet in the room when I suddenly felt my whole being filled with an indescribable Love. I looked away from her and said "I know you are pure Love, and Love could never allow such an experience to exist." I saw her about a week later and every evidence of disease was gone. She was radiant and strong. It was over!

So many healings have come on the heels of the Spirit challenging what we, as humans, must be holding in our hearts about God. We say one thing with our mouths, but accept horror in our lives, which denies what we say about the nature of God. Think about what you are facing right now. What is the situation saying about God? If it contradicts what you know is true...start your prayer there.

4) Ask God to clear away anything that would block your ability to know what Wisdom is directing. Once you know he only wants good...once you know that there is nothing in his nature that supports the pain and horror we accept in this life, and once you are determined to trust his wisdom over your own...then you must believe that he will "direct your steps." "A man's heart may devise his way but the Lord alone will direct his steps."[210] Believe it.

5) It is impossible to feel the intuitive impulse of Wisdom when you are still reacting to whatever is standing in front of you screaming about its power to destroy. So long as you are in a reaction, it wins. Only Wisdom can cause all human reactions to be silenced. "When the Lord speaks, the earth melts."[211] The most difficult step is the first one. You must pray for the grace of God to enable you to look away from this boastful, impertinent image and give your full attention to the surrounding glory of Mercy until it can be felt. Nothing, absolutely nothing can pen-

etrate this shield of defense. No matter how much time and attention it takes to get there and stay there...this is your answer. The power of this is available when we turn our attention to it. "Look unto me all ye earth and be ye saved."

6) If you are in a reactionary state over a conflict with another, so long as you are thinking about it, rehearsing it, talking about it...you are feeding the monster of division and strife. Everyone wants the conflicting parties to kiss and make up immediately, but I don't see the wisdom of that. It sounds like a religious rule to me. What I do believe is that you must keep silent and subdue your own spirit as soon as possible and then wait. Wait for Wisdom to speak. You never know what direction the wind will blow, because generally the cause of the conflict lies deep in the soul and it may be that your silence will be the catalyst to its discovery and removal. On the other hand, it may be much simpler than that and a deliberate and meaningful moment with the other party may be your wisdom. So like everything else, you must hold back, pause, with the specific intention of letting the Spirit go before you and declare its direction. The resolution may be immediate, but on the other hand, it may be years before a heart is humble and receptive to be able to resolve a conflict. In those cases, you must wait patiently for the Spirit to manifest this.

7) Even a reaction of joy can be detrimental to wisdom. There is a time for joy – but there is a time to hold it back until it is "wisdom" to release it.

As you can see there are no religious rules to follow. Instead we have a living, vibrant flow of sure direction available to us at all times that will "lead and guide us into understanding"[212] and elevate us to a receptive state where all goodness is our portion. This is the Holy Spirit of Eternal Life, and her voice is Wisdom. "It is to this man that I will look (to bless). He that is of a humble and meek spirit and that trembles at my Word."[213]

CHAPTER TWELVE

IS GOD THE AUTHOR
OF DARKNESS?

Did God have anything to do with what you are suffering? Many religions teach this. Even ancient religions, going as far back as the written word, contain this doctrine. They reason, if God is omnipotent, sovereign and supreme, then of course (he) must also be responsible for all human suffering.

I unequivocally disagree. First of all God is not a man capable of reacting and retaliating for our many offenses. This is vindictive theology and it is death producing. God is Spirit[214] and specifically, the Spirit of Eternal Life. This Spirit flows throughout eternity, creating visible manifestations of its very self. Since it is the substance of all it has "brought forth" then it also maintains and sustains what it has formed. It does this in an orderly rhythm, pulsating to the beat of its own Being. We see this as the systematic order of creation. The seasons come and go, day and night, seedtime and harvest all respond to this unbroken rhythm. The animals give birth at appointed times during the year. The gestation period never changes for each specific species. The moon has its cycle of appearing, the tide responds. The earth rotates on its axis as it circles the sun, all in its appointed fashion.

Mankind also has an appointed rhythm of life. To realize this and to respond to it is called wisdom. When a man orders his steps in wisdom, health and strength, prosperity and peace accompany him. But man has the option not to do so as well, unlike the rest of creation. Man can live his life in RE-action to his environment, his senses, his passions and desires, the demands of his body. Man can let all these things rule him and foolishly believe that he is in control, when in fact he is being governed by anything and everything. He does not direct his body, he doesn't know he can. He does not direct his emotions, he doesn't know he can. He does not "intend" specifically for his future, so he leaves his future up to the proverbial roll of the dice.

When he chooses to live in this realm of existence he is living under the law of cause and effect, or sowing and reaping. "Whatsoever you sow, that also shall you reap."[215] He is sowing to chance, so he reaps chance. He is sowing to a discordant rhythm, so he reaps confusion. This produces suffering.

The other option is responding to the current of the flow of the Spirit of Life within him, wisdom...and enjoying the benefits and rewards of such living.

Evil is a block in the flow of this Spirit which so blesses us. Evil is the result of upside down living, thinking and reacting. Evil is the result of fear. Fear of today, tomorrow, no certainty of goodness in the future. And fear is the result of not knowing that to respond to wisdom, will bring healing and blessing. When one realizes that being in the flow of this current of life can only produce goodness, all fear is dissolved. But fear acts as a magnet, attracting all manner of evil and suffering.

There is a difference between evil and the resultant suffering, and going through dark times in one's life. Darkness does not always mean suffering. Just as the little seed falls into the dark, damp earth, there to germinate, sprout and bring forth new life...we also must have our winter times, our night times, so that the new day, the new spring may appear. Jesus said new life appears after a "death."[216] But a death doesn't need to equate to suffering.

Death can be the death of a certain belief in order that a more pure understanding can come forth. Death can be a change of direction or circumstances in order for something new and fresh to appear. Daytime always follows nighttime. Springtime always follows winter. When you know that and you find yourself in a time in your life when there seems to be no life, say, the death of a long held dream, the end of a relationship, if you rest peacefully in the wisdom of knowing that new life is being forged out from the old and "I can wait patiently for this to pass" there will be no suffering. If you can look at the little seed and like it, know that the cycle of life will bring goodness out from this time, you are resting in wisdom, trusting the Infinite Goodness of the flow of the Spirit of Life...and all will be well.

However if you lack wisdom and understanding, if you are accustomed to re-actions and fears and non-trusting, you will find yourself in agony, wiggling and squirming all along the way. You must remember that "your life is not your own."[217] And that "no matter what" appears or ceases, your choice is to rest in your trust and love for "he who made you and swore his love and care for you."[218]

In Revelation the seven seals are lifted (removed) so that the Glory of God may be revealed through man. These seals must be lifted. These times are the winter months of our lives. If we can trust, if we can rejoice, if we can still sing and worship and rest...these times will pass swiftly and without suffering. But if we insist on specific outcomes, weary of the days, we will find pain and anguish.

Just as the day follows the night, just as spring follows the winter, just as the little seed brings forth life...this too shall pass and the "joy will come in the morning."[219]

"Although the fig tree shall not blossom, neither shall fruit be in the vines; the labour of the olive shall fail, and the fields shall yield no meat; the flock shall be cut off from the fold, and there shall be no herd in the stalls: yet will I rejoice in the Lord, I will joy in the God of my salvation. The Lord God is my strength. Habakkuk 3:17

Is this also true about sickness and disease? It is. The body cannot recover from dis-order, cannot regain the rhythm of order and life unless the entire neurological (nervous) system is at rest. That is why so many healings take place while the person is sleeping at night. Remember Jesus healed on the Sabbath and the word Sabbath means rest. When we are in peace, contentment, quietness and trust we are in the best position…really the only position to heal. That means no outlining. No visualization, no attempt toward manipulating God to make something happen your way. Trust the end result to Infinite Wisdom. That will be your wisdom..

I personally have experienced three specific time periods in my adult life where I felt I was placed on the "back side of the desert."[220] A very "dark night of the soul." The first time it happened I wiggled and squirmed, cried, prayed and found myself in a panic. But Wisdom finally raised her magnificent voice and I slowly began to understand. The daytime that followed was so remarkable, so fruitful and has stayed with me forever. It mapped out the course of my whole life here. So when it came around again, I at least knew that it would end one day and I just stayed as peaceful as I could. The last time I experienced my "winter time" I actually liked it! I had no fear that it wouldn't end and really didn't care whether it did nor not. And of course in due time it did. Wisdom finally took hold of my restless soul.

This is the resurrection principle.

CHAPTER THIRTEEN

PRAYER AND MEDITATION

There is no correct or incorrect way to pray. The wonderful thing about God is that every heart that turns to him is heard...saint or sinner. We can learn from the innocent prayers of the smallest child who gladly knows nothing about form or ritual.

It's not the way we pray, but the condition of the heart. It's not about how good we are or horrible we've been, but the humility and sincerity with which we approach God. Of all the things I have learned from God about God, the most life changing was the day I realized that "the rain falls on the just and the unjust alike, the sun shines on the unthankful and the evil alike."[221] So much for needing to "qualify."

I used to hear religious folks say that God doesn't hear the prayer of the sinner. Horrible words. I wonder how they think he would hear them then? Then there are those who have set themselves up as judges over what religious disciplines are legitimate and what is a "cult." And we all know that those who belong to cults are certainly never heard by God! Good grief! Of course not!

I like to ask God what he is all about. How he views a situation or event. How he feels about certain issues. I like it because I will believe what I hear from him a lot faster than the moldy doctrines of men. That helps me know how to pray or, better, what it is God wants me to receive from him. He doesn't take sides, for sure, but helps me to see all sides of an issue to have more compassion and greater wisdom.

Prayer is communication with God. It is listening as well as speaking. We too often talk but never wait for an answer. Mostly because we just don't think it will come. But it always does. Sometimes we need to just "stick with it" to finally understand what the answer is, but remember the words of your God, "Before you called I heard you and while you were still speaking I answered."[222] A good prayer is to learn to listen and to hear clearly. It gets to be a very lonely conversation otherwise.

I always start a prayer with exalting God. I always acknowledge something wonderful about him, his faithfulness, his mercy, his wisdom, his nearness. I do that to clear the atmosphere of chattering nonsense, of any fear or confusion...to get any problem out of my mind. It opens the way into the Presence of God, for sure. It opens my heart to be able to hear, as well. I don't just say words or "truths"...wouldn't that be sad if your very best friend responded to you in words of form and repetitive parroting of mostly meaningless words? What I say I mean.

God is good, only good, and I am always overwhelmed at his faithfulness and forgiveness and merciful love. I have never asked a question that has not been answered. Sometimes it takes awhile because I needed to grow in understanding before I could embrace the answer, but it always came. I have never asked for help that help didn't arrive. I have never asked for forgiveness that I have not felt mercy surrounding me. Even when I allowed my train to jump the track, Love has always gotten me back in the right direction, with no judgment or condemnation. All these years God has directed me sometimes down the most surprising paths, ones that I couldn't have ever imagined. My life has been enriched with a sense of fulfillment beyond most. My children and grandchildren are healthy, very blessed, and most of all they know where to go when problems or unexpected things come up. What in this world more than all this could I ever ask for?

So I start by remembering his goodness, much like Jonah finding himself in the "belly of hell"' and finally "remembering the Lord." I find a sense of gratitude filling my heart and a certainty that I stand in the Presence of the Most High God, who is intense Love and Mercy. With all that going on, there is no doubt that every encounter with God will prove to be fruitful and rewarding. I will receive.

People seem startled that when praying for another I don't rehearse whatever the situation is, or the person that is in trouble, to God. Why do they think I can bring darkness into the presence of Light? Why not exalt the Light and let it dissolve the darkness? All that the person who is troubled really needs is to feel the flooding Presence of Love engulfing them and every problem falls at their feet like so many chains that bind. Once I feel it while I am praying with them in mind, they also will feel it. Another proof of our oneness.

There are two atmospheres of thought…the place of confusion, chaos, pain and anguish, "biting and devouring one another."[223] It is from this realm that we take in all the diseases and other sufferings of humanity. The other atmosphere of thought is full of Light, grace, fulfillment, abundance and the glory that is God. To me, prayer is leaving one behind and entering into another. By doing so, the higher influences the lesser.

Jeremiah says many times that we are not to take our problems into the Glory of the Presence of God. "You shall not carry a burden into Jerusalem on the Sabbath Day"[224] (Moment of peace that always accompanies being in His Presence.)

Like Moses who needed to cover his face so that the Israelites would not behold the Glory of God in the state they were in[225]…once we also have spent time being filled with his glory, it will shine out from us without even knowing it, and it will influence the lives of anyone in our sphere of consciousness.

Like climbing Jacob's ladder,[226] we need to set a foundation that cannot be shaken. Our prayer life will change as we mature closer and closer to not simply praying to Jesus but to the revealing of Jesus Christ through our very souls. He starts out in our minds outside of us, different from us, always near and always attentive to us. But the goal is that we, our human identity, our sense of seperateness, and idiosyncrasies, dissolve as the Spirit of the Life of Jesus (the same Spirit that motivated him) occupies our entire being. Please take the time to read John, chapter 16, where Jesus is speaking to his disciples. They are sad because they realize that his human form will soon be leaving them. They think they will never see him again. But he says often to them that they will indeed see him again. Not floating down on a cloud or riding a literal horse in the sky as our literal friends are declaring. But through their very being. "He must increase and I must decrease."[227]

In John, Chapter 16, he likens the process to a woman who is in travail in childbirth. She, too, is bringing forth another life, right through her very being. He says that when the child is born (this is Revelation's "man child" in chapter 12) the pain will not be remembered "for the joy" she will now be able to experience. Then he says something that helped me to understand how all this is working...he said, "In that day you will not ask anything "in my name" again, for the Father will already know what you have need of"[228] and you will go directly to him, just as Jesus went directly to him while he walked this earth. More and more he is revealing himself (really the Spirit of his life) as us. More and more this is taking place, day by day. One thing that is noticed is that we will find ourselves in a much more intimate relationship with Infinite, Divine Love and Eternal Life, as our God...just as Jesus did. We will find ourselves deep in the Oneness that he then spoke of in the very next chapter, John 17.

So while we remain entrenched in our devotion to Jesus, we find ourselves truly "in him" and "as him." By necessity our prayers will take on a different tone. Instead of asking, we will be speaking as one truly sent from God and we will declare the absolute truth of every situation and expect to see the glory of Eternal Life demonstrated...just as Jesus spoke only truth and knew that his words would result in healings, deliverances, blessings and goodness to whatever the need.

Sadly there are those who hear these truths and assume that that is all that is needed. They rush to speak, affirming and repeating truths, giving the seed of truth no time to germinate, ascend, sprout forth and develop. "What went wrong," they ask, when failure stands looming before them?

The basic principle of all prayer is that the words, the sincerity of the heart, is led by the Spirit. It is the Spirit that knows the deep things of the heart. It is the Spirit that searches the marrow of the bones.[229] It is the Spirit that reveals what and when there are muddy waters in the way...such as unforgiveness, unresolved conflict or guilt, anger or defiance. It is the Spirit that reveals the purpose of the Father and the heart of the Mother. It is the Spirit that knows the way to success in every prayer.

Always, when someone asks for prayer or when I feel something that needs to be addressed, I pause and ask, "How must I pray about this?" When my heart is settled and I feel I have heard, then only do I proceed. Then it is the Spirit that does the praying and not the situation that is demanding the prayer. Will we let the Spirit, wise in counsel and deeply embedded in Mercy, lead our lives or will we let the various images of insanity of the chaos dominating this atmosphere of thought lead our lives? If so, we remain victims of the power of whatever appears.

And this brings us to meditation. What is it really and how is it attained?

In a way it can be described as communication with the vastness of Eternal Life without words or thoughts. It is a definite ascension into another realm of being and that is exactly what it feels like. It involves trust and a deep love for God, in that, we simply go to receive. We have no wants, needs or demands that we take with us. We will receive whatever Wisdom deems good. Long ago we left behind any nonsense of evil, so we go expecting the wonders of the Glory of God to meet us and envelop us.

Something we read or hear may so inspire us as to "open the way" to such an experience. Or we may simply determine that is what we want to experience so we make the way.

We can be sitting or reclining with a deliberate intention of meditating. We can be walking along, working, tending to our lives or even dreaming...and Love invades the space and something clearly is being revealed. Meditation goes both ways.

If we are engaging in silent, deep meditation, we might choose absolute stillness and quietness, not moving our bodies, not thinking our thoughts...or we might choose soft music without words that would distract us. When the thoughts of confusion come, simply go back to your intention and don't worry about them. They are not coming from you anyway. Soon they will stop because you will have ascended far enough out of the world of confusion and entered deeply into the realm of goodness and grace where those thoughts cannot occupy.

It is the heart of God and the heart of man, joining as one...for one we truly are. It is the Song of Solomon's two lovers meeting just to join in love as one being. There is no hidden agenda, nothing specific to gain, except all of paradise, of course. It may last a second, as it often does when I am about my daily life. It may last hours, as long as I choose when I am intentionally engaging.

So, you see, there are many aspects of prayer, many levels, so to speak. All are a gift from Infinite Love to us. None are to be despised. We will experience all of them in any given day. We go up and down Jacob's ladder continually...and all that is good. The important thing to remember is that it is between your heart (not your mouth) and the heart of God.

Different religious disciplines may approach prayer in differing forms that you might meet along the way. Again, each one has the same purpose and intention, to communicate with God, therefore they are not to be categorized or judged.

What a privilege is prayer! How I made my first twenty-five years without it is a mystery, except that God knew me long before I knew him. So again, "I am found of those who knew me not."[230] What a heart of tender mercy we have encountered! There is not a storm, not a flood, not a drought, not a disaster in any life that prayer, deep, humble, sincere prayer will not avail. There is no question, no confusion, or guidance that will not be found in prayer. It is our life line. Our umbilical cord of oneness.

Just as no book should presume to tell you how to love, no one can tell you how to pray. There is no formula, only desire.

It will cause us to reconnect with our original state of Eternal Life. It will reveal Paradise. Right here. Right now.

It is the blueprint to Life.

REFERENCES

CHAPTER ONE

1   Matthew 25:34
2   Matthew 6:10
3   Revelation 21:1
4   Leviticus 18:21
5   Luke 8:10
6   Proverbs 25:2
7   Revelation 1:6
8   Genesis 1:12
9   Genesis 2:17
10 2Corinthians 4:18
11 Job 36:24
12 Ephesians 2:10
13 Matthew 9:29
14 Proverbs 23:7
15 Romans 1:20
16 Psalms 19:1-3
17 John 1:4
18 John 1:9
19 John 1:16
20 John 17:22

CHAPTER TWO

21 Matthew 8:12
22 Genesis 3:24
23 Matthew 9:17
24 Acts 2:17,
    Hebrews 8:11-12

CHAPTER THREE

25 Proverbs 4:7
26 Revelation 3:16-17
27 1 Thessalonians 5:3
28 Romans 2:4
29 2 Timothy 2:13
30 Revelation 2:6
31 Mark 2:16
32 Matthew 23:24
33 John 16:13
34 Hebrews 8:11
35 Ephesians 1:4
36 Job 38:7
37 Psalms 90:1-2
38 John 1:4, 9

92 Genesis 1:9

93 Hebrews 11::39

94 Genesis 1:12

95 Hebrews 8:10-12

96 Mark 11:24

97 Romans 8:19,22

98 Isaiah 64:6

99 Luke 17:10

100 Matthew 22:11

101 Revelation 19:9

102 Revelation 14:4

103 Proverbs 29:2

104 John 9:7

105 1 Corinthians 15:53

106 1 John 5:18

107 John 6:44

108 Isaiah 26:20

109 Psalm 30:5

110 Revelation 1:4

111 1 Corinthians 15:28

112 Colossians 3:3

CHAPTER SEVEN

113 1 Corinthians 15:47

114 Genesis 28:12

115 Matthew 11:15

116 Genesis 3:24

117 John 16:13

118 1 John 5:6-8
      John 16:13

119 Genesis 1:12

120 Psalm 24:1

121 Ephesians 2:10

122 Colossians 3:11

123 Romans 3:4

124 Ecclesiastes 7:29

125 Proverbs 4:7

126 John 16:13

127 Proverbs 5:15

128 Colossians 2:22

129 Genesis 2:17

130 John 10:10

131 Genesis 1:2

132 Habakkuk 2:14

133 Isaiah 1:18

134 John 10:28-29

135 1 Corinthians 15:56

136 Matthew 9:29

137 Proverbs 23:7

138 Job 22:21

CHAPTER EIGHT

139 Philippians 4:6

140 James 4:14

141 Romans 11:36

142 John 12:24-25

143 John 3:8

144 Luke 18:19

145 John 3:30

146 Matthew 6:5

147 Matthew 5:36
148 Matthew 17:5
149 Psalm 37:4
150 Psalm 21:2
151 Matthew 5:45
152 Exodus 20:8
153 Isaiah 6:8
154 John 10:3,5
155 Revelation 14:4
156 Psalm 37:4
157 Romans 10:17
158 Leviticus 19:36
159 John 5:30

CHAPTER NINE

160 Luke 2:7-9
161 John 5:30
162 John 5:30
163 Revelation 24:5
164 Acts 16:25-26
165 Jonah 2:2
166 Daniel 3:19-25
167 Matthew 14:19-21
168 Philippians 4:6
169 1 Thessalonians 5:18
170 Philippians 1:6
171 Psalm 37:4
172 2 Samuel 6
173 2 Chronicles 20
174 Psalm 100:4

CHAPTER TEN

175 1 Corinthians 15:45
176 1 Corinthians 15:53
177 Matthew 3:8
178 Matthew 11:11
179 John 15:16
180 Isaiah 43:1
181 John 15:16
182 John 12:24
183 Matthew 8:5-10
184 Isaiah 45:22
185 Jeremiah 17:21
186 Revelation 21:5
187 Revelation 21:5
188 Exodus 20:8
189 Isaiah 30:15
190 Psalm 23:2-3
191 Isaiah 45:2
192 Revelation 3:8
193 Hebrews 13:5
194 John 3:8
195 Ecclesiastes 1:7
196 1 Kings 7:7
197 Revelation 2:17
198 Isaiah 42:2
199 Revelation 2:17
200 Isaiah 43:18-19
201 Revelation 3:12